CIVIL JUSTICE AND THE JURY

CIVIL JUSTICE AND THE JURY

Charles W. Joiner

PRENTICE-HALL, INC., ENGLEWOOD CLIFFS, N. J.
1962

Library of Congress Catalog Card No.: 62–17565

Printed in the United States of America

13481—C

FOREWORD

Freedom and justice for the individual—grounded upon a just system of laws and protected by the courts—are the keystones of America's strength. This is the American concept, and it is our main claim to moral leadership in the world community.

However, the real test of our system is the extent to which our ideals are given actual concrete reality in the lives of our people. A system of laws—however just—that exists only in theory is a slim basis for a claim to moral leadership. It is a weak reed to support our national strength. We must not forget that the role of the courts is not merely to define the right; it is also to administer the remedy. Unless the remedy is actually applied to persons and things, the right is merely a pious idea.

With these thoughts in mind, we are challenged to re-examine our system of justice to determine whether it is based upon sound procedures and systems, and whether we are presently approaching or receding from our goal. That purpose is well served in this study of *Civil Justice and the Jury*.

Nowhere does Government touch the lives of the people more intimately than in the administration of justice, and nowhere is it more important that the governing process function with efficiency and common sense. Nothing we can say or do is so important as the way we administer justice. And when I say *we*, I mean the lawyer and the layman, too.

The courts represent the one institution which has been entrusted in a peculiar way to our keeping—lawyer and layman alike. It places a tremendous obligation on us to make our federal and state systems work, for without an efficient judiciary, there can be no real justice. It is primarily the law and its adequate and fair administration that makes individual liberty possible.

The men and women who are called upon to serve on juries in both our federal and state courts have maintained a standard of fairness and excellence throughout the history of our country. They have demonstrated a vision and a will toward the administration of justice that is a wellspring of inspiration. It is, therefore, with confident anticipation of their continued service as jurors, and with the highest respect for our jury system, that I welcome this further analysis and study of the history and operation of the civil jury in our country.

PREFACE

It is appropriate that a Canadian member of the International Academy of Trial Lawyers should write the preface to this work, because in most of the Canadian Provinces with the exception of Ontario, the civil jury has ceased to exist for practical purposes. In Ontario, there are more civil jury trials than in all the rest of the British Commonwealth nations. England, the home of the civil jury, calls upon its citizens to do jury duty today in no more than two per cent of civil cases, and it is unlikely that Canadian civil juries will survive this generation, except in rare cases. And all of this has happened since the First World War.

This is not the place to analyze the various causes of the disappearance of the civil jury throughout the Commonwealth, but we who have lost our civil juries can more readily appreciate that loss and sound a note of warning to our American brethren before the forces giving rise to the abandonment of the civil jury become overwhelming.

Once lost it is unlikely the civil jury will ever return, and for a multitude of reasons. One of the most important of these is that a civil jury trial makes necessary special skills on the part of our judges and lawyers, skills which can only be developed and retained through constant experience in civil jury trials. The common law of a country is found in the clear and simple statements of judges to juries. There is a constant obligation to make this law understandable to laymen to keep it from becoming a complex system of rules only understood by a select group in the community, but not every lawyer is capable by way of experience of doing this. In the United States there is a most competent Bar experienced in the trial of civil cases before a jury. Let that Bar fall into disuse for as little as a generation through abandonment of the jury system, and the jury system could never be revived because the new generation of lawyers would not have the experiential skills necessary to place the law and the facts simply enough before a jury of laymen to enable them to arrive at a satisfactory verdict. The reservoir of talent would be gone. In Canada and the Commonwealth we have such a new generation of counsel already. Untrained in jury technique, they have no desire to try cases before a jury.

The loss of the civil jury in the British Commonwealth and the attack upon it presently being made in the United States has prompted the International Academy of Trial Lawyers to sponsor this work on the American Civil Jury, the object of which is to enlighten the American people about the working of one of its oldest forms of dispute resolution in the belief that an informed public opinion is best able to decide whether the civil jury should survive. The Academy was fortunate in prevailing upon Professor Charles Joiner of the University of Michigan Law School to undertake the work. After an active career at the Bar in the trial of lawsuits, Professor Joiner has devoted himself to the study of trial methods and is today one of the leading exponents of the American trial process and its constant development. His purpose was single-minded: it was to bring to the American people the story of the civil jury, freely discussing its advantages and disadvantages, and whether the disadvantages could be removed or alleviated or, at worst, were reason for the abandonment of the system.

Professor Joiner has fulfilled his purpose and completed a careful study of the civil jury. His views are not necessarily those of the Fellows of the International Academy; in fact, some of them find themselves in disagreement. Of course, the provocation of disagreement is the inevitable hallmark of any scholarly work. Here, in one volume, layman, student, social scientist, can find the arguments for and against the civil jury system, together with copious references to source material if he wishes to pursue his studies further.

If the civil jury is to survive, it will be because of the faith of the American citizen in a system of justice that brings his independent fellow citizens into the resolution of his disputes.

Edson L. Haines, Chairman
Continuing Education Committee
International Academy of Trial Lawyers

CONTENTS

INTRODUCTION

The jury is one of our oldest and most deeply rooted institutions. To many it is the most revered of all. Like legislative government and the court system, the jury is protected in most constitutions and antedates all of these constitutions by centuries. It has been eulogized by judges and lawyers in terms more glowing than have been applied to any other institution; yet, in the twentieth century, it is under severe attack from many sources In two of our greatest states, New York and California, responsibile public officials have suggested its abolition in certain civil cases, and the American Foreign Law Association doubts that there is justification for it. Most of the problems arising in litigation are laid at the feet of the jury.

What are the facts about the jury? How do the arguments, pro and con, balance out? The University of Chicago Jury Project, conducted by University of Chicago faculty members and financed by the Ford Foundation, is finding and reporting facts about the jury. These reports, some of which have not been published, reveal information about the jury not known before, and tend to support those who argue for the retention of the institution.

Now, however, there is a need to examine the jury as it operates today, to compare the arguments pro and con, to marshal what is known about its operation, to put it in context within the whole framework of government as well as within the social process of resolving disputes between litigants, and lastly, to examine suggestions for its improvement.

Also, it would be helpful to examine what thoughtful lawyers and judges have said about the jury since its inception. This book, then, is first a critique of the jury today, and second, a collection of thoughtful statements about various aspects of the jury made by observers during the past 200 years. It is not, nor does it purport to be, based on new research or new facts. Its purpose is limited: to help laymen understand and think about issues involving the jury—issues with which they may soon have to grapple.

Charles W. Joiner

PART ONE

THE JURY
IN CIVIL CASES

I

THE JURY: A JUDICIAL AND SOCIAL INSTITUTION

COURTS: THEIR FUNCTION

Man is a busy and gregarious animal. He has developed a complex civilization and culture that throws him into intimate contact with other men. But no matter how highly developed that civilization and culture is, problems arise that cause disputes, disagreements, brawls, and wars. These have always been a part of man's history.

Dispute resolution

The Old Testament, purporting to trace the history of man from its beginning, is a record of constant strife, dissension, invasion, and war. Plato, deploring the friction existing among men made an effort to chart the ideal society. The Romans, although their civilization was highly developed, finally fell as a result of internal bickering and external conquest. Throughout the Middle Ages man built fortified castles to defeat the ceaseless efforts to subject him and those for whom he was responsible. Conflict, dispute, and ambition are a vital part of England's history also, having created a vast number of problems ultimately solved by warfare or under the English common law. The history of this country has similarly not been free from strife resulting from thoughtlessness, ambition, pride, and greed. Men died in the conquest of the West because of their desire to own virgin land and to protect property which they felt belonged to them. More recently, armed conflict has raged between unions and corporations.

Wherever man comes into contact with other men, disputes will arise which need resolution. These disputes may be between individuals, involving such minor issues as the cost of a meal or the quality of an automobile; or they may be disputes between nations which result in war.

Society has long understood that if it is to survive, conflict must be kept to a minimum and ways must be found to resolve disputes amicably, in a manner that is agreeable to society itself. Finding these ways has become one of the major functions of government, making it possible for people to live ever closer together, and for a single individual to be in contact with hundreds of other individuals each day of his life. *Dispute resolution is a major governmental obligation.*

The principal method of resolving disputes that arise between individuals is through the use of the courts. Courts are state agencies created with the primary function of resolving disputes. Courts normally consist of the following persons: (1) a judge, either elected by the people or appointed by a responsible person in government for a term of years, for life, or for good behavior; (2) lawyers, tested by the state according to standards of education and proficiency set by the state, who are selected by litigants for a particular case pending before the court; (3) a jury, in many cases selected randomly from the public at large; (4) a court reporter, responsible for writing down, either in shorthand or by mechanical means, a verbatim record of everything that goes on in the courtroom; (5) a court executive or bailiff, usually a deputy sheriff responsible to the judge, having as his principle function, the keeping of order and the execution of the judge's commands in the courtroom; and (6) a clerk, whose job is to keep track of the papers used in the court.

Courts are unique in that they are empowered to settle disputes between individuals, not upon the application of some state officer, but upon the application of an individual. In other words, a citizen of this country can submit his dispute with another citizen to a court and require that the other person also submit that dispute to the court for resolution. Persons can resolve their problems without the use of courts, but courts and their power to resolve a problem can be invoked by any one person even though another who is involved does not desire to have it solved. The means of dispute resolution in modern society then (1) may be invoked by one party, (2) may involve compulsion on the part of the other party to submit the dispute to the court, (3) does not require the advance permission of government officials, and (4) may be had in official government agencies, called courts.

Without courts or some substitute for them government would fail, for courts ultimately enforce all of the laws of the state. Three examples will be given to illustrate this statement. (1) The law of a state says that a contract entered into by two individuals is binding upon the parties and should be performed. The purpose of this law is clear: it is to provide a way in which agreements can be used as the basis for our economic structure. (2) The law says that a person should conduct himself at all times as an ordinary, reasonable, and prudent person would under like or similar circumstances, and if he fails to conduct himself in this way he must pay damages of an amount sufficient to compensate an injured person for the injury done. The obvious purpose of this law is to provide reasonable security for a person and his property. (3) The law says that a father shall support his children who are under legal age. The obvious purpose of this law is to provide a reasonable device of responsible support for the children so that society does not have to assume these burdens.

But what happens if a contract is not performed, or a

person does not act as an ordinary, reasonable, prudent person, and causes injury to another, or a father does not support his child? In the absence of any court system or other means of resolving disputes, we would be left to barbaric, forceful methods and the strongest of the lot could act with impunity. *The law would fail for lack of any responsible agency recognized by society to resolve the disputes arising between individuals. There would be in fact no law and no government.*

Courts resolve disputes between individuals, between them and legal institutions, between these institutions themselves, and between government and legal institutions or individuals. The last of these is descriptive of our criminal law and is beyond the scope of this discussion. Here we are interested in the jury as an institution in civil cases—that is, disputes between individuals or between legal institutions created under state auspices, such as corporations.

Although one of the principal functions of the court is to resolve disputes between individuals, by no means is it essential for the resolution of these disputes. There is nothing magic in the court device. Many other methods and agencies have been used in our history and are currently used in other parts of the world.

Fight or threat of fight. In man's early history disputes were largely resolved through fighting or threatening to fight. Even today, small children resolve their problems in this way, and those who have grown in body but who have not yet matured resort to this means of resolving their disputes. When disputes involve national entities, we have war. In most instances this method of dispute resolution is invoked because of an absence of, lack of knowledge of, or lack of confidence in, a binding method of resolving the problem otherwise. Certainly no responsible citizen today could claim that this method of dispute resolution is proper. In a sophisticated society right doesn't always have might.

Referee. A referee is used today in sporting disputes. As

such he usually needs to have a first hand knowledge of the rules of a game and is not usually adapted to fact-finding in the absence of this knowledge. The complicated problems arising from commercial transactions and from people living together in populated areas clearly do not fit the concept of a referee. Normally his power comes from the consent of the parties and if this consent is lacking, or if confidence in the referee is destroyed, the referee's ability to resolve problems facing him utterly fails. If, on the other hand, the referee has greater powers than this coming from the state, he has another name, that of judge.

Commission. Commissions consisting of several persons are often used in the resolution of today's international disputes. Their authority comes from agreements between the governments creating them. Normally their powers are distinctly limited, usually to reporting facts which are found and recommending results. Binding authority is usually lacking and, invariably, there is no power to enforce their findings.

Administrative Board. A great number of special problems of society are decided by administrative boards and commissions. These bodies are usually charged with the exercise of legislative and executive as well as judicial powers. Examples of this type of body are the Workmen's Compensation Boards, the Unemployment Compensation Boards, the corporation boards, the public service boards, and the labor boards. In most instances these boards are charged by law with bringing to the decision process a built-in legislative bias in favor of a policy established by law.

Expert panels. Occasionally disputes arise over quality or over causation. When this is true, it is not inconceivable to invoke experts in the resolution of these disputes. A problem arises in that no machinery has been devised yet which will put the sanction of the state behind the panel's decisions. Perhaps the reason that this machinery has not been developed is because in most fields of knowledge there are different schools of thought and constantly developing ideas which some experts are more likely to believe than are others. And so within the panel, we see the same basic dispute as that between the litigants. Also, disputes arising between individuals very seldom involve only the narrow points on which the experts' judgments would be helpful.

Mediators. As the term "mediator" implies, there is no power in such a person to bind the parties to his judgment. His task is to attempt to reach agreement, and when the parties are unable to agree the mediator fails. He is at a loss to proceed if the parties are adamant.

Arbitrators. Arbitrators are recognized in many states today as a valid means of resolving disputes, usually with the consent of the parties. They are used to a considerable degree in the commercial world and in the resolution of certain labor-management disputes. The shortcomings of this device are that the consent of both parties is required and that adequate means have not yet been developed for checking on the standards applied by the arbitrators in the dispute resolution process.

Judge. The judge is a state-appointed officer specifically charged with obligations in connection with dispute resolution. He has a long history of dispute resolution powers in equity cases. He has the full power of government behind his decisions. In equity cases he decides on the basis of fact and law, applying the law to the facts to reach a conclusion. Appeal to another judge or group of judges is the means recognized by the law of checking on the correctness of the judge's decision.

Judge and jury. This double-headed agency is the method commonly accepted in this country for resolving civil disputes. Its long history, dating back more than 500 years, provides its stability and acceptance by the public as a means of dispute resolution. The jury is selected on an *ad hoc* basis from the public at large, participating in dispute resolution as the agency which decides what the facts are and applies to those facts the legal doctrines stated by the judge. The advantages of this form of dispute resolution are many: (1) it is generally accepted by the public; (2) the division of authority between judge and jury provides a system of internal checks and balances within the trial process itself; (3) it is more accurate and fair in the application of general standards or rules of law; (4) there is less chance of background prejudice in the fact-finding process; (5) it permits citizen participation in government; and (6) it lessens the chance of unduly expanding bureaucracy in the dispute resolution process.

Of these methods, the judge and jury is the method having the longest history and the greatest acceptance in the United States. The civil jury is enshrined in the Constitution of the United States and in most state constitutions. The Seventh Amendment to the Constitution, for example, is couched in these terms:

> *In suits at common law, where the value in controversy shall exceed twenty dollars, the right of trial by jury shall be preserved, and no fact tried by a jury, shall be otherwise re-examined in any court of the United States, than according to the rules of the common law.*

Similar language is found in state constitutions. Truly the civil jury as a means of resolving civil disputes is an American institution.

Increased need for dispute resolution

The importance of courts in today's society is increasing because dispute resolution is becoming a more significant part of government, one that is more greatly needed than ever before in our history. Which method of resolving disputes is superior involves the consideration of a number of factors.

First, the population of this country is increasing rapidly. In 1940 the population of the United States was 131,669,-

275; in 1960 the population was 179,323,175, a 36.1% increase. Necessarily then, people are living closer together. This is accentuated, however, because the greatest increases have come in the areas already metropolitan. In these metropolitan complexes we find a vast increase in population and hence in the many problems created with people living closer together. Individuals have more dealings with one another; tempers get shorter. It stands to reason that 100 people living in one building will have more disputes and problems than 100 people scattered over 100,000 acres. Thus, added to the facts that we are now greater in number and living closer together than ever before, it necessarily follows that we are more litigious than ever before. Disputes among individuals needing resolution in courts are increasing even more rapidly than population. Courts are becoming more and more crowded and complaints are being lodged against certain of these courts for delays in resolving some of these disputes.[1]

During the past 40 years we have seen an expansion of the rights of man never before witnessed in history. When Thomas Paine spoke of the rights of man he was speaking of the rights of man against government. But in the first half of the century, the rights of man against man have been completely reevaluated. In the nineteenth century, for example, very few courts recognized any significant right of privacy—that is, the right of one citizen against another citizen to damages in the event that the second citizen wrongfully invaded the privacy of the first, either by taking or publishing pictures, writing stories, or by other means. Now, this right of privacy is generally protected by law. Hence, the rights of one citizen have been greatly increased; and the obligations of others have correspondingly been increased. Years ago there was no right to recover for pre-

[1] In 1960 the attention of the American Bar Association was directed to this problem when its Ross Essay topic was "What New and Improved Methods of Administrative Supervision Would Aid in Reducing Delay and Congestion in Trial Courts?"

natal injuries. Today many courts recognize this right and award damages against a wrongdoer. *Necessarily, as rights increase the obligations of others increase. This concomitant increase in rights and obligations likewise has the tendency to increase substantially the disputes arising between individuals, thus increasing the work of the courts.* All this has become a part of our constantly *changing concept of social consciousness, the recognition of the value of the individual, and the fact that people constitute our greatest natural resource.* Courts have tended to protect against invasions of personal liberties. Whenever rights and obligations are increased, there will be more litigation, for there necessarily will be more disputes. Thus more people living closer together and having more rights and obligations has increased the litigation in our courts.

In addition, these newly developed rights, as well as many of the older, established rights have relied primarily on indefinite standards to define acceptable conduct. *The civil rights and liabilities of parties are determined by the application of rules of law having no black and white connotation, but rules using meaningful but indefinite words to describe appropriate or inappropriate action.* The law is full of words like "reasonableness," "ordinary, reasonably prudent man," "reasonable notice," "reasonable time," reasonable belief," "care of the locality," "reasonable opportunity to reject," "reasonably intelligent person," and "reasonable suspects." *Words such as these permeate all phases of the law and rely upon the community to write their complete definition in each case. The law has refused to write with fixed definitions that are applicable to all cases, but instead has used general words to indicate the standards of conduct imposed upon people. Why should this be so? Because it would be arbitrary in many instances for the law to attempt to be more definite.* The law uses the general standards of the community as a way of being less arbitrary. *It is important then in the application of these standards that the community have a part in the application of their definitions in a given case.* This factor is relevant in determining the place of the civil jury in the solution of disputes.

The developments in science and the advances in engineering are changing the size and character of problems placed before the courts. Problems are becoming more complex and larger in scope, making wise solutions even more imperative than in the past. With the slingshot and the buggy, wisdom and community acceptance were important ingredients in dispute resolution; with the gun and automobile they are imperative.

To summarize then, fair and wise dispute resolution is an important aspect of the job assigned to courts and is becoming even more important as each day goes by. The means by which the courts carry out this function must be scrutinized to a large degree from the viewpoint of which method of dispute resolution will be more sound, more fair, and more acceptable by the general public.

A sense of fairness—Due process

A second function of courts is to develop a sense of fairness among people. Courts are a part of government, the part of government involved in resolving disputes. Corrupt courts may decide disputes in the same way that fights decide disputes, but corrupt courts fail since they do not show fairness in government. Mistakes and biases in dispute resolution, in the same way bring courts and government into disrepute. Our constitutions, state and federal, require "due process of law." We now hear of the "rule of law" from a great many thoughtful commentators. By this, something more is meant than the following of detailed, prescribed procedures. Most of us, and the courts today concur, believe that a fair result is somehow implied in these phrases. Since courts are the major agency through which due process and the rule of law is brought home to our citizens, courts are significant factors in the development of a sense of fairness and fair play among them. Obviously this can be developed only if the courts decide cases fairly, and in a way recognized by all as being fair. However, justice and fairness are only part of the whole. The climate must be such that the results, fair though they may be, will be generally accepted over a period of time by the citizens of this country. It becomes important therefore that people everywhere believe that courts are fair and just and have confidence in the fact-finding process. This is another factor having a bearing on an ultimate decision on the best method of resolving disputes in our courts, and any decision which is made as to the place of the jury in this process must in the long run be weighed not only on the scale of fairness but also by the criterion of popular belief and acceptance that decisions are fairly decided.

Courts make law

The last major function of the court is that of law-making. In the deciding of disputes the courts are often called upon to formulate standards of conduct. In the formulation of these standards courts will, on many occasions, be unable to pinpoint any prior decisions or legislation. The dispute must be solved and since there appears to be no defined standard, the court has to create a standard by which to judge the dispute. This standard, once enunciated, becomes a precedent for further decisions and a guide for conduct in the future. This is law as much as that passed by legislatures.

Courts: Their need and function—Summary

Why is it so important to spend so much time in a discussion of courts when our subject is the civil jury? Why must we examine the function of courts? All of this is important because in order to analyze the civil jury and to assess its value, we must understand and appreciate what courts do, and what they are intended to do. If, for example, justice and fairness in dispute resolution were not a significant part of our concept, we could as well have trial by battle. If we could eliminate the need on the part of the public to believe that government has provided a sound and just means of dispute resolution and if this were not a significant part of the obligation of the courts, we could as well determine disputes by a flip of a coin. Until we put the function of the jury in context with the full function of courts, we cannot accurately assess the value of the civil jury.

JUDGE AND JURY

When a jury case is ready for trial, it is assigned to a particular court. Under the guidance of a judge, names of jurors, originally chosen from a cross section of the community, are drawn by a court officer and the jurors are questioned by the lawyers or the judge to determine their fairness and lack of bias. Those who appear biased are challenged and excused from the case. Twelve are finally accepted as the jury and are sworn to try fairly and impartially the issues in the case.

Both lawyers are permitted to explain to the jury and the judge what their case is all about. This is called an opening statement. It serves the basic function that the picture on the cover of a jigsaw puzzle serves for the person attempting to fit the pieces together. The opening statement gives a relatively complete picture of the facts of the case as seen by the lawyer describing them. This permits the jurors to have an organized look at the case in advance. When the evidence is introduced, the jury will be able to fit together the various bits and pieces into an intelligible whole. After the opening statements, the lawyers are permitted to introduce their evidence.

First the evidence for the plaintiff is produced, mainly through the interrogation of witnesses who tell what they know about facts relevant to the issues of the case. In addition to this, documents or other exhibits having a bearing upon the issues may be produced. The defendant's lawyer may cross-examine each witness or challenge the documents as a means of testing the correctness of the assertions or the validity of the documents. It is the judge who determines whether or not the evidence shall be received.

After the plaintiff's evidence is produced, the defendant's lawyer follows a similar procedure. The plaintiff's lawyer is given the right to test by cross-examination.

After all the evidence has been submitted to the jury for their consideration, each of the lawyers is permitted to summarize his contentions in a final statement before the jury. Each lawyer attempts to demonstrate why his witnesses should be believed, why his theory of the case has been proved, and the logic of his contentions. In other words, the lawyers at this point are assisting the jury in analyzing and sifting all of the various evidential pieces that have been brought before them.

Following these final arguments, the judge instructs the jury on the law either by reading or speaking extemporaneously to them the rules of law applicable to the issues in the case and the facts as brought out by the parties to the dispute. It is from these instructions that the jury is finally apprised of each issue to which it must direct its attention and is told of the applicable standards that must be used in deciding these issues.

Having heard the facts, having been assisted by the lawyers, and having been instructed on the law, the jury retires to a private room to consider its verdict. The jury's obligation at this point is to resolve the fact disputes, apply the legal doctrines which the judge has mentioned in relation to them, and bring back a verdict in favor of the plaintiff or defendant. This verdict is the basis for the court's final decision which is called a judgment.

The significant differences between a trial before a judge and jury and a trial before a judge alone are these: (1)

when a trial is before a judge alone and there is no jury impaneled, the public is not brought into the case and the obligation of decision rests upon the judge's shoulders; (2) in a trial before a judge alone there is no adequate way to detect unconscious bias or prejudice on the part of the judge and to challenge him for it since lawyers cannot conduct a *voir dire* examination of the judge as they do the jury; (3) when a trial is before a judge alone, he is not obliged to state publicly the propositions of law on which he relies in determining the case as he must do when he instructs a jury; (4) the decision by a jury on the facts is reached after deliberation and discussion, whereas a decision by a judge is by a single man without the advantage of discussion with others; (5) the decision of a jury is made by persons usually representing a cross section of the community, and this a judge cannot do. These are differences that may be significant to discerning persons in dictating a choice in modes of trial.

The relationship between the judge and jury in the trial of civil cases should be examined in terms of: (1) the process of decision, fact, and law, and (2) the process of checking and balancing each other.

Decisions on fact and law

As has already been seen, there are two major aspects to a rational dispute resolution. First, there is the decision as to the correct law to be applied, and second, there is the finding of the facts in the case and the application of the law to those facts. In the typical trial by judge, the judge is obliged not only to determine the law but also to find the facts and apply the law to those facts. In a jury trial, on the other hand, there is a division of authority. The judge determines and states the law and governs the trial. The jury, on the other hand, finds the facts and applies the law as stated by the judge to those facts, thus reaching an ultimate conclusion or verdict. In determining which is the best means of proceeding in a given case, the qualities of each of these agencies should be examined in light of their duties.

Presumably the judge is a skilled professional lawyer. He is supposed to know the law, or at least to understand the law when it is explained to him by the lawyers in a case, and to be able to state it accurately and succinctly. On the other hand, the judge is not a cross sectional representative of the community. The members of the bar do not come from a cross section of society and those of the bar who are called to be judges do not even reflect a cross section of the bar. The judges are likely to be highly skilled people who at times are somewhat removed from the feelings and desires of the people of the community. They are experts in law determination. On the other hand, the jury has no particular expertise in law determination. The members of the jury are not lawyers. They are not to determine the law themselves, but to accept the statement of the law as given them by the judge. They do, however, come from a cross section of the community. Although they do not have any particular expertise in fact determination, they more closely represent the desires of the community.

Since each case has different facts, professional fact-finders are of less value than are professional law finders. The law to be applied in different cases may be the same, but fact questions are never the same in different cases. There is no need for previous knowledge of the facts of other automobile cases to find the facts in a particular automobile case. In fact, just the contrary may be true. The prejudices of the previous automobile cases may seep into a fact determination of a second case if a person or group of persons continually are obliged to make fact determinations in similar cases.

Two important issues stand out: (1) the place of background prejudice in fact decision-making, and (2) the place of deliberation in such a decision. These questions will be discussed later.

Checks and balances

The division of function between judge and jury creates a system of checks and balances built into the typical jury trial and unique in our system of judicial administration.

Jury decisions on facts and the application of law to facts seem to be an ameliorating influence on the trial process. The harshness of legal doctrine is often softened by the jury. I do not think we should consider this idea as a strong reason for sustaining the jury, but if it is impossible to make the law less harsh—and I think it is impossible at times to soften a law simply by writing it more accurately and with more definition—we ought to have a system for trying lawsuits that will tend to mitigate the harshness that we otherwise are unable to eliminate.

We have seen in Michigan how over a period of ten years the jury of the community tended to apply the indefinite standards of the law along the line of community desires. Some years ago, but within this ten year period, the Supreme Court of Michigan was constantly reversing trial judges for failure to direct verdicts in cases involving contributory negligence. This meant that in cases in which the Supreme Court said that there ought to be a directed verdict as a matter of law on the ground of contributory negligence, the trial juries were bringing in verdicts in favor of the plaintiff, even though they were properly instructed on contributory negligence. The Michigan Supreme Court went through a metamorphosis a few years ago in connection with this problem. I cannot say whether the moth turned into a butterfly or the butterfly into a moth, but there was a very great change in the attitude of the court. For a number of years the Supreme Court has been constantly reversing the trial judges for directing verdicts in too many cases involving contributory negligence.

In the first instance we found juries wanting to apply a community standard. They had a tendency not to hold a plaintiff one hundred per cent responsible when there was only contributory negligence. In later instances we have found that the juries return a number of verdicts for the defendant when the court is not directing them. The latest study in Detroit showed that there was a substantially higher number of defendants' verdicts after this change. So the jury can work to relieve the harshness at both ends. Although the new view may seem harsh, the jury tends to ameliorate this by taking the middle ground. This was true in earlier cases as well, for the jury then tended to take the middle ground also.

The judge, through his power to set aside unreasonable and unwarranted verdicts, protects against the harshness of unconscionable juries. There is no reason to believe that every jury will reach a God-given result. Juries will make mistakes, therefore this judicial power to set aside verdicts at the trial level provides a judicial check on the jury.

Historically, the power of the judge to set aside the verdict for insufficient evidence, or because the verdict was harsh or unreasonable, arose from a desire to save the jury system. In about the middle of the fifteenth century the practice of putting jurors in jail when they made mistakes ceased. The judges assumed the power to deal with the problem directly by setting aside the verdict when juries made mistakes. There arose a great cry against some of the decisions that juries were making at that time, and the jury system was saved only by providing a check upon them, a check that now is not widely used, but available.

It is this mutual check that brings the judge and the jury together in such a way that they can function effectively in the trial process by joint agreement rather than by subordinating one to the other.

Checks and balances in the jury system are effective in two other ways: (1) the judge can help the jury with its fact-finding processes by instructing it; and (2) in difficult cases, a jury decision can take the pressure off a single judge. The latter is more common in criminal cases, where we know that there is going to be one result or the other. It is always wise, as far as the public and the administration of justice is concerned, to have the decisional process involve the jury as well as the judge, because this gives much more support to the decision.

LAWYERS AND THE JURY

The jury cannot be fully understood without some consideration of the role that lawyers play in a jury trial. Our trial proceedings are adversary in nature. The theory on which such a trial system is based is something like this: if the plaintiff is obligated to bring before a fact-finder all the proofs favorable to his side, and a similar obligation is given to the defendant, that fact-finder will have before him at the time of decision all the facts relevant to the case without having prejudged the case in his search for evidence. This is particularly true if we add to this the State's power to compel witnesses to attend and testify, and to compel evidence to be brought before the court on application of either party. Such a procedure necessarily results, if pursued diligently, in all evidence being brought forward. Moreover, since the fact-finders have not been involved in bringing the evidence forward, presumably they have no prejudice.

The alternative to this, which has been rejected by the Anglo-American legal system, is for the judge or fact-finder to involve himself directly in bringing evidence before him. The most recent example in this country of this type of proceeding has been the procedure followed by many Congressional investigating committees, where the committee itself has been involved in bringing forward the facts, listening to the evidence and then basing conclusions upon these facts which it, itself has produced.

The long history of the success of the adversary system, as exemplified by the Anglo-American method of trial, makes attack on the adversary system very unlikely indeed. Even critics of the jury do not directly attack the adversary system of trial.

Lawyers play a distinct part in this adversary system. As the representatives of the litigants the burden falls upon their shoulders to marshal the facts and to bring them before the judge or jury in a convincing way. The whole series of ethical canons which apply to lawyers is an effort to outline the obligations of lawyers in light of this adversary system. The lawyer is obliged to serve the indigent prisoner. He is prohibited from serving clients with conflicting interests. The lawyer cannot assert his personal belief as to his client's innocence or the justice of his cause. But he does owe "entire devotion to the interest of the client, warm zeal in the maintenance and defense of his rights, and the exertion of his utmost learning and ability to the end that nothing be taken or withheld from him save by rules of law legally applied. No fear of judicial disfavor or public unpopularity should restrain him from the full discharge of his duty." A lawyer is required to treat witnesses and litigants with fairness and due consideration. He should not act as a witness for his client. He should not attempt to influence the court through the press, or in private consultations. He is required to conduct himself before the court with candor and fairness. He should not curry the favor of juries with fawning, flattery, or pretended solicitude for their personal comfort, but he does have the obligation of controlling the trial to protect his client's rights. He must respect the confidences of his client; in talking to witnesses, he must scrupulously avoid any suggestion calculated to induce them to suppress or deviate from the truth. He must disclose to the court any fraud or deception that he finds to have been practiced on it. As an advocate he speaks for his client.

The jury too relies on the lawyer. Not only is the lawyer

responsible for the order in which the facts are presented to the jury and for the manner of examination and cross-examination of witnesses, but the jury relies upon the lawyer for a clear statement of the case in his opening statement and for a clear and careful summary of the case in his closing argument. Lawyers in this respect help and teach the jury. After listening to both sides, the jury is in a position to decide the case.

Perhaps the most difficult problem for a layman to understand about the posture of the lawyer arises in criminal cases but carries over into civil cases as well. The question involves the defense of a person who admits to the lawyer that he is guilty. I am indebted to a friend and former student of mine, F. Hubert Mather, for the following succinct statement on this point. I commend it to you.[2]

> *From a practical standpoint, the role of being an advocate becomes perhaps the most difficult when a client has admitted a set of facts to the lawyer which, in the opinion not only of the lay-client but of the lawyer, clearly constitutes the crime charged; or, when a client, fully understanding the charge, says "I'm guilty but I want to plead not guilty and I want you to defend me." I should make clear, however, that a lawyer is under no obligation to represent this man and can quite properly tell him that he doesn't care to take the case. It is a breach of no obligation to suggest that he consult other counsel. The difficulty would only become serious if he did take the case or was under court order to do so.*
>
> *Assuming that the lawyer for one reason or another finds himself in this situation, you might well wonder how he could handle it and still fulfill his moral obligations to himself, the court, and his client. In my readings on this subject I learned that the Shanghai Bar Committee requested the Council of the English Bar to ex-*

[2] Mather, "The Nature of Advocacy as a Profession—and Some Problems." Excerpt from a paper read before the Lansing [Michigan] Torch Club, November 16, 1960.

press an opinion some years ago for the guidance of counsel on the question "the propriety of counsel defending on a plea of not guilty a person charged with an offense, capital or otherwise, when the latter has confessed to counsel himself the fact that he did commit the offense charged." In response to this the Bar Council suggested first of all that three essential axioms be kept in mind: "(1) That every punishable crime is a breach of common or statute law by a person of sound mind and understanding; (2) That the issue in a criminal trial is always whether the accused is guilty of the offense charged, never whether he is innocent; (3) That the affirmative rests on the prosecution." The Bar Council went on to say, "the ways in which this duty can be successfully performed with regard to the facts of the case are, (a) by showing the accused was irresponsible at the time of the commission of the offense by reason of insanity or want of criminal capacities; or (b) by satisfying the tribunal that the evidence for the prosecution is unworthy of credence, or even if believed, is insufficient to justify a conviction for the offense charged; or (c) by setting up in answer an affirmative case."

The Bar Council went on to say "confession of guilt by the accused to his advocate does not release the advocate from his imperative duty to do all he honorably can for his client, but such a confession imposes very strict limitations on the conduct of the defense. An advocate may not assert that which he knows to be a lie. He may not connive at, much less attempt to substantiate, a fraud. While, therefore, it would be right to take any objection to the competency of the court, to the form of the indictment, to the admissibility of any evidence, or to the sufficiency of the evidence admitted, it would be absolutely wrong to suggest that some other person had committed the offense charged, or to call any evidence which he must know to be false having regard to the confession, such, for instance, as evidence in support of an alibi, which is intended to show that the accused could not have done, or in fact had not done the act; that is to say an advocate must not (whether by calling the accused or otherwise) set up an affirmative case inconsistent with the confession made to him. A more difficult question is within what limits, in the case supposed, may an advocate attack the evidence for the prosecution either by cross-examination or in his speech to the tribunal charged with the decision of the facts. No clearer rules can be laid down than this, that he is entitled to test the evidence given by each individual witness, and to argue that the evidence taken as a whole is insufficient to amount to proof that the accused is guilty of the offense charged. Further than this he ought not to go."

THE AMERICAN CITIZEN AND THE JURY

The judicial and social institution of the jury must be examined in its relationship to democratic government and the place of the citizen in the process of government. Americans, as much as any other people and perhaps more than all others, have traditionally distrusted authority. This has been evident, I think, since America's independence. The Revolutionary War, involving, superficially at least, taxation without representation and denial of the authority of a select few to make laws, is evidence of a distrust of central authority. Our federal system of government with divided responsibility between national, state, and local governments indicates a similar distrust; as does the Tenth Amendment to the Constitution which, although not greatly implemented, reserves the powers of states, and also the Bill of Rights, which protects individuals against the central government.

The jury is a vestige of nonprofessional government, an institution in which nongovernmental people play a significant part in the governmental process. Here private citizens on an *ad hoc* basis exercise part of the dispute resolution responsibility of government, thus minimizing any biases of governmental bureaucracy. It is popular because it gives private citizens a broad participation in government. A significant job is performed without hiring new governmental employees or creating a new hierarchy. The jury provides for citizen participation in government unequalled elsewhere. If democracy is really to work—and it has worked pretty well for 170 years—our citizens must not only be informed at election time but must know the meaning of making responsible decisions. Through the jury more private citizens participate in responsible decision-making than in all government put together. Certainly the decision of a juror is a responsible one, and he realizes it; and when he has seen the difficulty in making it, he cannot help but understand some of the problems that others, such as government officials, face when they have to make even more significant decisions than his. However, responsible decision-making by jurors is possible only when they have the qualifications for decision-making. The major impediment to responsible decision-making has to do with these qualifications, or rather a lack in them. I suggest that juror quality is something to which we must direct a great amount of attention. Perhaps a lack of juror quality causes some of the problems for which the jury as an institution is being criticized. I shall discuss this later in connection with methods of strengthening the jury.

THE JURY AS A DELIBERATIVE BODY—EXCHANGING IDEAS, ARGUMENT, AND DISCUSSION

In dealing with this subject we begin to uncover a fundamental reason for the continued use of the civil jury. The civil jury consists of twelve persons, and a unanimous or near unanimous verdict is required in all states. A verdict, either for the plaintiff or the defendant, requires something more than a vote by the members of the jury unless the case is very clear indeed. Exchange of ideas, argument, discussion, and deliberation are invariably required. A single fact-finder (the judge) could misunderstand some evidence. He might not think the question through in an appropriate manner so as to arrive at a truthful result. Moreover, all judges probably have an amount of background bias in the decision-making process as a result of the accumulation of experiences up to that time. Unless our decision-making process provides some means for deliberation, argument, exchange of ideas, discussion, and for attempts to convince others of the correctness of one's thinking, these biases and mistakes would never become known and an erroneous decision might be put upon the books. It seems obvious that if there is the opportunity for discussion, exchange of ideas, argument, and deliberation, a number of the biases and most of the mistakes will be brought out into the open and, being exposed to the light, will lose their controlling significance.

The jury is a deliberative body. It does discuss, argue, and exchanges ideas before it can report a decision. Therefore, it is not unfair to assume that the decision which it reaches may have fewer mistakes and fewer biases involved in it than would such a decision made by a single person.

This is documented by a number of psychological studies carried on during the past 20 or 30 years. Most of these studies involved not juries but other small groups with decision-making tasks. They shed light on the soundness of intuitive judgment in the deliberative process of decision-making. The studies indicate that group decisions are fairer, more efficient, and more accurate in fact-finding than are the decisions of an individual. The give-and-take of group deliberation screens out errors, negates biases, and eliminates erroneous hypotheses to a far greater extent than individual deliberation. It was found that the interaction during deliberation was the crucial difference that made group decisions more just than a pooling of individuals without the give-and-take of deliberation.[3]

For example, an experiment was conducted in which witnesses to an apparently genuine accident were produced.[4] The comments of the individual members of the jury, after hearing the witnesses, were compared with the deliberative results of the jury as a unit after discussion. The final report of the jury covered only those points agreed upon unanimously, and although it was not as complete as were the reports of the individuals, it was significantly more accurate. In summarizing this experiment, it was stated: "Thus although the requirement of unanimity apparently reduced the number of items accepted for the jury report, it reduced the number of errors even more." [5]

Many reasons have been suggested for this: that the group tends to sway toward the majority opinion; [6] that judgments converge as a function of group interaction; [7] that deliberation results in a more critical examination.[8] Whatever the reason, the results provide sound statistical evidence that small groups similar to the jury, when allowed to discuss problems openly, have a marked tendency to decide these problems more skillfully than individuals. This adds significant weight to the arguments of those who defend the civil jury. For, whatever other characteristics prove a need for the retention of our jury system, its chief

[3] Gurnee, "A Comparison of Collective and Individual Judgments of Facts," 21 J. EXP. PSYCHOL. 106–112 (1937); Timmons, "Decisions and Attitudes as Outcomes of the Discussion of a Social Problem," CONTRIB. EDUC. No. 777, New York Teachers College, Columbia University, Bureau of Publications (1939); Thorndike, "The Effect of Discussion Upon the Correctness of Group Decisions, When the Factor of Majority Influence Is Allowed For," 9 J. SOC. PSYCHOL. 343–362 (1938).

[4] Dashiell, "Experimental Studies of the Influence of Social Situations on the Behavior of Individual Human Adults," HANDBOOK OF SOCIAL PSYCHOLOGY (ed. Murchison) 1097–1158 (1935).

[5] Kelley and Thibaut, "Experimental Studies of Group Problem Solving and Process," HANDBOOK OF SOCIAL PSYCHOLOGY (ed. Lindzey) (1954).

[6] Thorndike, *op. cit.* note 3.

[7] Sherif, "A Study of Some Social Factors in Perception," ARCH. PSYCHOL. No. 187 (1935).

[8] Shaw, "A Comparison of Individuals and Small Groups in the Rational Solution of Complex Problems," 44 J. AM. PSYCHOL. 491–504 (1932).

function has always been to decide disputes; if it does this more effectively than an individual, any differences in time or cost, if indeed they exist, must be considered insignficant.

This effectiveness is a much desired characteristic of civil juries since accurate solution of a small number of important issues is the most important aspect of the decision-making process which they engage in. Furthermore, as will be discussed later, in the section on strengthening our jury system, if a verdict required more than a simple majority but less than complete unanimity, even more issues could be decided by the jury with fewer errors than an individual judge would make.

At one time it was felt that groups were superior in the decision-making process because of the influence of the ablest member of the group,[9] but doubt was cast upon this idea by the use of a homogeneous group.[10] This study indicates that group decisions are superior to those of individuals not because of the influence of the ablest member but rather because of the greater interest and involvement of group members. In the group process remarks by each individual are exposed to the criticism of other members and thus there is a feedback and stimulation, forcing members to be more cautious and self-critical. Groups have greater critical resources than individuals working alone; they are able to see more. Thus the study found that "A more objective view of the problem resulted from competition between the private prejudices of group members." [11] In other words, a person with one value orientation would try hard to find errors in others, and the biases of the individuals would tend to be less controlling.

Once an individual has a given mental bias or a particular way of looking at the problem, some outside information or

[9] Watson, "Do Groups Think More Efficiently Than Individuals?" 23 J. ABN. PSYCHOL. 328–336 (1928).
[10] Barnlund, "A Comparative Study of Individual, Majority, and Group Judgment," 58 J. ABN. PSYCHOL. 55–61 (1959).
[11] *Ibid.*

stimulation is usually necessary to shift it. "For an individual a wrong set once established may make it impossible to solve the problem." [12] There is an abundance of evidence that sets or biases have a tendency to persist, preventing objectivity.[13] So an individual, a judge, with his built-in set of personal prejudices finds it more difficult to make a critical and objective examination of the facts before him, while a small group, a jury, is able to weigh the biases of each individual to a far greater extent and arrive at a decision in which these biases are virtually nonexistent. Individual members change their opinions as a result of social influence, the rational arguments put forward, and the strength of the individual initial opinions. The good or correct seems to win out over the bad or incorrect. Biases seem to disappear.

Sometimes group members reach immediate unanimity and there is a tendency not to question the solution. In this case the product will be inferior because it will never have been subjected to the test of deliberation. But it must be remembered that a group of twelve jurors will rarely, except in a clear cut case, reach unanimity through a consensus taken at the outset, which prevents deliberation. A judge, however, once confident in his original hypothesis may forever be prevented from re-examining it even though it is latently erroneous. All that is necessary to set the deliberative process in motion in a jury is for one or two members of the twelve to interpret some of the facts differently from the other members. With their hypothesis challenged the others will defend themselves and the vital deliberation will take place. This being so, the jury will invariably have to deliberate prior to arriving at a solution, and as we have seen, once deliberation takes place the erroneous hypothesis is removed, errors are screened out, and biases are destroyed.

[12] Taylor and Faust, "20 Questions Efficiency in Problem Solving as a Function of Size of Group," 44 J. OF EXP. PSYCHOL. 360–368 (1952).

[13] Cf. the Gestalt psychologists in general, especially Asch, SOCIAL PSYCHOLOGY (1952).

A substantial amount of work has been done on the identification of the factors which contribute to the superiority of group decisions over those of individuals. The presence of an audience, the type of problem being solved, the size of the group, the attractiveness of members of the group to each other, and the initial attitudes of the individuals in the group, have all been found to be significant in determining how effective the group will be.

An audience seems to have a bad effect upon the validity of group decisions; an audience, passive or active, seems to provide a social stimulation that may interfere with individual problem-solving as well as that of a group. This would seem to indicate the need for juries to continue to carry on their deliberation in the privacy and secrecy of the jury room. It was also found that an anticipated future audience will lead an individual to decide in terms of what he thinks the particular audience will want.[14] Thus a judge deciding a case as an individual will be motivated to some extent by his awareness of the courtroom reaction while a jury deliberating as a group will be more involved in achieving harmony within the group.

Of course, whether or not groups perform better than individuals in problem-solving depends in part upon the kind of problems to be solved and the kind of decisions to be rendered. Barnlund's study [15] indicated that when a problem involving personal prejudices is complex and not intuitively obvious, the group will be superior to the individual in the process of decision-making. This is due to the greater critical resources available to the group, the effect of countering prejudices by discussion, and the fact that individuals alone may only be capable of getting part of the answer. An earlier study [16] had found in group deliberation more interaction

[14] Grace, "Effects of Different Degrees of Knowledge About an Audience on the Content of Communication," 34 J. Soc. Psychol. 111–124 (1951).

[15] Barnlund, *op. cit.* n. 10.

[16] Deutsch, "Task Structure and Group Process," 6 Am. Psychol. 324–325 (1951).

and attention to each person's contribution in a human relation problem than in a puzzle problem. This may indicate that when unanimity is required or when the problem is complex, more critical resources are made available. These two studies are of real significance in relation to the jury because in every instance its decision involves problems of human relations, and more often than not the jury's problem is quite complex and not intuitively obvious.

It does seem that for most tasks with which a jury or a judge can be involved, the jury functions better than the judge. But where the problem is more technical or scientific, such as deciding whether a thirty-foot skid of a car indicates a certain speed, the specialist, or a group of specialists, will be better, since even among specialists group deliberation brings critical resources which overcome the biases of the group's members.[17]

As to the size of the group to be used in decision-making, an increase in size, up to a point, would bring forth more ideas as well as increase the identification of more active members and the consequent danger of them controlling the decision. There is no real evidence, however, as to the exact size of the most effective group for the decision-making process. The evidence does indicate that a group larger than three is required and that it must be small enough to provide the give-and-take of group discussion. Perhaps we are fortunate that juries number twelve, for this seems to be well within the limits for effective deliberation, although a smaller number, perhaps six, might be timesaving and less costly without hindering the decision-making process. This point is discussed later as another means of strengthening the jury system.

The relations among members of the group have some bearing upon the decision-making process. Friendships inhibit group effectiveness insofar as they divert energy from

[17] Taylor and Faust, *op. cit.* n. 12; also Asch and the Gestalt psychologists, *op. cit.* n. 13.

the task of decision-making to social matters. However, it also assists the decision-making process insofar as it allows easier interaction and communication. It may, however, increase the homogeneity of opinion and thus hinder full consideration of any issue. It was found [18] that as group cohesiveness increases, its power over the members increases. What this means is that as the attractiveness of the group to the members increases, i.e., as the members' desire to remain in the group increases, more pressures toward uniformity of opinion arise. Therefore, when consensus or unanimity is a criterion for ending the problem-solving process as in a jury situation, the increase in the cohesiveness of the group creates pressure toward uniformity of opinion. This is a drawback to the unanimity requirement but does not of itself militate completely against the requirement. For this reason I feel that total unanimity in jury decisions can be dispensed with, thereby strengthening the jury.

It might be interesting to observe the effect of previous attitudes held by the members of the group and brought to the group from the outside. Whether or not an initial attitude is a result of personal experience or of the group standard, it will resist change either from within the group or outside if it is strong. As a result of press comments and the buildup of prejudice in a law case, initial attitudes of great strength may be built up which are difficult to change in the group. Of course, attorneys for the litigants try hard to prevent an individual who they think is obviously prejudiced from being impaneled on the jury, whereas a judge with a similar amount of prejudice, or in fact even more, would not be disqualified. The results of deliberation, however, may bring about a change in the attitudes of those jurors ultimately selected, a change that might not otherwise be brought about in its absence.

[18] Festinger, Schachter, and Back, SOCIAL PRESSURES IN INFORMAL GROUPS (1950).

Two early studies[19] found evidence that the more complex and broadly based the facts presented to the group were, the more accurate the opinion arrived at was apt to be. Marston studied the judgments of jurors after they had heard a story from a number of witnesses. The data suggested that there were certain advantages to having several witnesses: (a) to extend the range of observation, thus increasing the completeness of the jury's survey, and (b) to provide checks and contradictions in the testimony, thus enabling the jurors to increase the accuracy of their judgments through detecting erroneous testimony.

One would expect, and there is slight supporting evidence, that the opinions of individuals whose status is high, because of intelligence, class, expertise, etc., would be more respected by other members of the jury group than those of a low status person. This would apply to witnesses as well as fellow jurors, and would result in the jury's assigning greater weight to the judge's actions and statements in the courtroom.

Psychologists agree that procedures which facilitate minority expression, communication in general, and the exchange of ideas, are very desirable in helping the group decision-making process. This too seems to be a justification for the secrecy, privacy, and intimacy of the jury room.

After an examination of these past experiments on group decision-making, one cannot but doubt the thoughtfulness of persons who would destroy the civil jury instead of improving it. These critics claim that the jury is arbitrary, causes court congestion, is an unnecessary expense, is the cause of the burdensome rules of evidence, and is responsible for the excessive number of legal errors. It is doubtful that these criticisms, which will be discussed later, are valid. But even if there is justification for these objections, their significance

[19] Jenness, "The Role of Discussion in Changing Opinion Regarding a Matter of Fact," 27 J. ABN. SOC. PSYCHOL. 279–296 (1932); Marston's study on testimony is cited by Dashiell, *supra*, n. 4.

is slight when faced with the results of the social and psychological surveys discussed above. When it is seen that small groups are more capable than individuals of rendering decisions free from error, from personal prejudice, and from erroneous hypothesis, and when it is remembered that the function of the jury is to make decisions on disputes being litigated, the only conclusion to be drawn is that the civil jury is necessary and highly beneficial to our legal system and that the logical course of action is to improve this body, not to destroy it because of a few easily-corrected shortcomings.

Particularly when we consider the effect of background bias on decision-making does the jury deliberation take on real significance. We all know that lawyers are biased in many matters, some in favor of plaintiffs, some in favor of defendants. This is not to say that lawyers are not objective, but that as an individual each lawyer starts from a hypothesis that is a little different from that with which his neighbor starts. This happens largely as a result of repeated handling of certain typical claims and of constant exposure to problems seen from a single viewpoint. This constant exposure to the typical problems of his clients tends ultimately to bias his thinking to such an extent that the bias is difficult to overcome. When lawyers become judges, the biases which they had as lawyers are carried over. All good lawyers and judges have some background partiality. It cannot be eliminated, for the best lawyers are probably the most partial. We must, however, reduce the effect of this bias in a system of dispute resolution.

The method of trial by jury which results in a decision based on the deliberation of the jury reduces these preferences and aversions. First of all, the set or bias acquired by the lawyer-judge is not actively carried into the jury room; it does not directly affect jury decisions. Secondly, the jurors are not professionals; they do not hear cases day after day; they do not develop the same kind of set that judges develop from hearing the same kinds of cases, one after another. They are a nonprofessional, nonpermanent group, therefore, they are likely to have much less bias for or against certain kinds of cases, or persons than does a judge who sees particular kinds of persons or cases in court day after day. Each juror, of course, has individual partialities which have been developed at home or at work, but they are not enhanced by being repeatedly involved in similar cases as are many lawyers and judges. Thus, I think that a jury will tend to approach the problem with less bias than a judge and the deliberative process of decision-making used by the jury will reduce even further that partiality. What remains is likely to be an honest reflection of the community from which the standards of conduct come which are involved in the dispute.

THE JURY AS THE CONSCIENCE OF THE COMMUNITY

In this section I will try to show that the jury has a second significant function that can be served in no other way than by drawing a number of persons from the community at large. This is the function of acting as the conscience of the community in dispute resolution. "Conscience of the community" involves bringing a cross section of the community into the process of dispute resolution. An understanding of the ideas involved in this section necessitates an acceptance of four major premises. When these are accepted, I think the conclusion is inevitable:

1. The jury as we know it is drawn from the community at large. Although the methods of selecting it vary from state to state, and even though the official charged with selecting the jury may be different within the same state, in almost all of our states the locality in which the court is sitting is responsible for furnishing a certain number of jurors to hear civil and criminal cases. All the suggested proposals for jury

reform provide for community cross-sectional representation on the jury. To a varying degree juries throughout the United States not only come from the community, but they also represent all aspects of that community even though there are still a number of problems in connection with the breadth of the jury base. These need to be ironed out and will be discussed later.

2. The judge is also selected from the community. Normally he comes from the actual community in which the court is sitting, although in a great number of states he rides circuit and may be sitting in counties adjacent to the one in which he actually resides. This is simply a compromise to the expediency of judicial business. Nevertheless, it is true that the judge comes from a community similar to those in which he sits during his circuit riding. His background, however, does not make him a representative of the mean or median of that community. Although he may deny it, he probably comes from its elite since he is a lawyer and since lawyers are normally members of the more educated group of a community. The lawyers of a community are its leaders. Not only are judges taken from a body of these lawyers but they are usually chosen from the better ones. In other words, they are selected from the elite of an elite. Certainly, this kind of judge is needed in our system of judicial administration for solving many basic problems of law demands a man learned in the law and with the capacity to understand its fine points. On the other hand, it is equally true that the judge is generally not in a position, because of personal background, to be representative of the mean or median of the community.

3. Most laws are written in very general terms. This is true whether the laws are derived from judicial decisions or from enactments of the legislature. They may seem to be definite at first glance, but on closer examination almost all laws have very general provisions incorporated in their terms. For example, it is unlawful to drive in the state of

Michigan at a speed in excess of 65 miles per hour. This seems to be very definite indeed and the question of fact that might be presented to a jury would be whether or not a person was driving faster or slower than 65 miles per hour. But there is a further provision in the same law. It is not always lawful to drive 65 miles per hour since it is also not lawful to drive faster than is reasonable and proper under all circumstances. This is language in general terms, which needs interpretation. This imprecise language needs application in the light of facts presented in a given case. Language of this kind is used in our statutes and is found in our common law not only because the English language is imprecise but, more importantly, because the ideas conveyed by this language were not fully crystallized by the persons who created them. Rather than risk the harm that might develop from the use of precise terms in situations in which such terms were not applicable, our legislators have used general language, relying upon others to interpret and apply the terms to particular cases. It is often impossible to write with more precision than is done in statutes in common law.

4. The law requires community-wide acceptance. If the community as a whole did not accept law, people would be very unhappy. There could be widespread disregard for or even revolt against the government that created the law. If government is to serve society, law must be close to an accepted standard of the community. We have seen, for example, how the disregard for prohibition caused irreparable harm. We are seeing today how in many areas our lottery laws are completely out of step with the desires of the people. When people begin to feel that some laws are to be disregarded in the community, the same disregard may be carried over to other laws. If this continues the end result may be a breakdown of government.

These four premises, that the jury comes from the community and is a reasonably fair cross section of that community, that the judge is an expert coming from the elite of the community, that the law is often very general in its terms, needing precise interpretation and application in individual cases, and that it needs to have strong popular support in the community itself, lead inevitably to the conclusion that the litigious process must somehow involve the community and that the jury is probably the best device possible to bring out this community spirit, this community consciousness of the law. Imperfect as the jury system may be, it is far better than having harsh, rigid standards that are not perfectly applicable to a case before the court, or having an unsympathetic member of an elite interpret the laws. It is the jury that helps resolve disputes in accordance with a law which it has interpreted in a way that will maintain popular support for it and the legal system, thus helping to build and shape the application of general laws in a way that will be widely accepted.

Almost 100 years ago, Mr. Justice Hunt, speaking in support of a unanimous Supreme Court of the United States, expressed this thought:

> . . . *Twelve men of the average of the community, comprising men of education and men of little education, men of learning and men whose learning consists only in what they have themselves seen and heard, the merchant, the mechanic, the farmer, the laborer; these sit together, consult, apply their separate experience of the affairs of life to the facts proven, and draw a unanimous conclusion. This average judgment thus given it is the great effort of the law to obtain. It is assumed that twelve men know more of the common affairs of life than does one man, that they can draw wiser and safer conclusions from admitted facts thus occurring than can a single judge.*[20]

[20] *Railroad Company v. Stout,* 84 U.S. 657, 33 S. Ct. 529 (1873).

II

DEVELOPMENT OF THE CIVIL JURY

An effort to assess the value of the civil jury should rely very little upon historical background unless this background has direct bearing on contemporary matters. Such a study as this should rely instead upon current attitudes, criticisms, and values rather than those of hundreds of years ago. For this reason my sketch of the development of the civil jury will be very brief. For those who desire more, a great many legal scholars have written treatises on the history of the civil jury which are available in all law libraries.[21]

HISTORY

Almost all civilizations at one time or another permitted laymen to participate in the process of deciding disputes between litigants. In England after the Norman conquest, however, the participation of laymen in dispute resolution became formalized, thus forming the basis of our modern civil jury.

Society was not always so sophisticated as to be able to determine facts from a presentation of evidence or the testimony of witnesses. For centuries trial by battle was an accepted means of resolving disputes. Also, for many years

21 Cf. Lesser, HISTORY OF THE JURY SYSTEM (1894); Forsythe, HISTORY OF TRIAL BY JURY (1875); Busch, LAW AND TACTICS IN JURY TRIALS (1949).

the ordeals of fire and water were used to resolve disputes. Then, William the Conqueror introduced the Norman institution "inquisitio" into England, permitting certain persons to demand an inquest to render judgment in certain defined matters. This was not initially used in civil matters, but it did contain the germ of modern trial by jury since it examined facts. In the twelfth century statutes were enacted expanding the right of individuals to have questions aired before the king. These statutes, describing in some detail the situations in which this "jury" could be convened, are the basis for the modern civil jury. Although trial by battle still continued, other means to ascertain right gradually became popular among the more sophisticated people of that time. Their procedures are not altogether clear to us now, but we do know that they were not inflexible, but varied a great deal. Very soon a substantial number of disputes were being submitted to the twelve persons who were chosen to resolve them. Originally the persons chosen were those who had knowledge of the dispute, but later it became proper for such a jury to summon witnesses, and when this became the accepted way of resolving disputes it also became appropriate to excuse those jurors who had knowledge of the dispute on the ground that they might have predispositions in the case. It was decided that the case should be resolved on the testimony or the evidence presented to an open-minded jury. Thus the procedure of challenging unqualified jurors became recognized.

Jurors served under the guidance of a judge. At an early date jurors who returned a wrong verdict were severely punished. Later, when it became obvious that the punishment of a hapless jury would not correct the wrong, the verdict was set aside and a new trial granted. When the jury began to hear the testimony of witnesses and to consider evidence, a number of rules were developed to assist them in considering only that evidence which was relevant and competent. These rules have developed over the years into a substantial body of law called the law of evidence. When the American Constitution was written, specific guarantees were placed in it pertaining to jury trial. We shall discuss these subsequently, and explore the constitutional meaning of the term "jury trial."

DEVELOPMENT OF EQUITY

At the present time not all disputes in the courts are resolved by juries. In some disputes, called equity or chancery matters, there is no right to trial by jury. These must be decided by a judge. The development of this branch of law began as one of the greatest legal accidents of all times. Since the reign of Henry II, during which the first statutes were passed giving real basis to the right of jury trial, courts have existed in England on a national scale. Life during Henry's time was not so complex, and justice was very crude indeed. Then, the right to use the courts was derived from the "purchase of a writ." These writs became very numerous and after a period of time, in an effort to simplify matters, it was ordered that no new kinds of writs could be framed. England, however, developed into a nation of commercial substance instead of remaining a strictly agricultural nation. The complexities of the law therefore increased. New rights were being urged before the courts without there being any way for the courts to react to them since there were no more writs to be used to get a new case before them. Courts refused to hear disputes that did not fit within the accepted writs. In such a situation, the person who was harmed often appealed to the king through the chancellor, who, acting on behalf of the king, dispensed a great deal of justice. This official called people before him by summons, and inquired into the nature of the dispute; he resolved disputes and ordered wrongdoers to do their victims justice. Therefore, king's courts handled certain kinds of disputes and the chancellor handled other kinds of disputes. Disputes in the king's courts required a jury, while those decided by the chancellor did not require a jury. Gradually, the trial of disputes by the chancellor became more formalized and a whole new court of chancery or equity was established. Thus, two systems of courts were resolving civil matters.

When the British began to settle in America, this dual court system was transplanted here. For over 100 years an effort has been made in this country to abolish distinctions between law and chancery, and only recently has this been accomplished in most of our states. The major distinction between them, however, still exists—that of the right to jury trial. It is only in those cases where historically the three great common-law courts of England would assume jurisdiction that there is a right to jury trial today.

Many treatises have been written on the distinctions between law and equity, and on the definition of equitable relief.[22] Obviously, in this short paper nothing could be accomplished in trying to outline the distinctions between the two. Basically, however, law has awarded money damages after the happening of an event; i.e., after an automobile accident, an injured person can sue for damages. Equity, on the other hand, has been much more prone to give relief prior to the happening of an event, in order to prevent harm or wrongdoing by ordering people to do or refrain from doing certain acts. In the former case the jury trial is a matter of constitutional right, but the latter is to be decided by the judge without a jury.

THE CONSTITUTION, THE SUPREME COURT, AND THE JURY

In this complex country, with a central federal government and fifty separate state governments, it is difficult to generalize about the jury. There are, however, a number of common grounds upon which it can be discussed.

[22] Joiner and Geddes, "The Union of Law and Equity," 55 MICH. L. REV. 1059 (1957).

First, most states have a specific constitutional provision concerning the jury which is worded somewhat like this: "the right to jury trial shall remain inviolate." This provision and those like it apply to state courts and have no effect upon the federal courts.

Secondly, in the Constitution we find the following provisions having bearing on the right to jury trial:

> *In all criminal prosecutions, the accused shall enjoy the right to a speedy and public trial, by an impartial jury of the State and district wherein the crime shall have been committed, which district shall have been previously ascertained by law, and to be informed of the nature and cause of the accusations; to be confronted with the witnesses against him; to have compulsory process for obtaining witnesses in his favor, and to have the assistance of counsel for his defence. (Sixth Amendment)*
>
> *In Suits at common law, where the value in controversy shall exceed twenty dollars, the right of trial by jury shall be preserved, and no fact tried by a jury, shall be otherwise re-examined in any Court of the United States, than according to the rules of the common law. (Seventh Amendment)*
>
> *Section 1. All persons born or naturalized in the United States, and subject to the jurisdiction thereof, are citizens of the United States and of the State wherein they reside. No State shall make or enforce any law which shall abridge the privileges or immunities of citizens of the United States; nor shall any State deprive any person of life, liberty, or property, without due process of law; nor deny to any person within its jurisdiction the equal protection of the laws. (Fourteenth Amendment)*

Obviously, by their terms the Sixth and Seventh Amendments apply to federal courts. The question of whether they also apply to the states through the Fourteenth Amendment will be discussed later.

THE JURY IN FEDERAL COURTS

Meaning of jury trial

When our Constitution was adopted, the jury was a reasonably sophisticated institution in England. It was thought so highly of by the framers of the Constitution that two of the provisions of the Bill of Rights were devised specifically to protect the right of citizens to a jury trial, the Sixth Amendment in criminal cases, and the Seventh Amendment in civil cases. Significant aspects of trial by jury have been discussed by the Supreme Court in defining the more general terms found in these Amendments. In the 1899 case of *Capital Traction Co. v. Hof*,[23] which was appealed from an inferior tribunal, the question was raised whether a constitutional trial by jury could be held before an inferior tribunal. The opinion of the Supreme Court in this case added substance to the Seventh Amendment. The Court held that a constitutional trial by jury required the jury to be in the presence and under the superintendence of a judge empowered to instruct them in the law, to advise them on the facts, and to set aside their verdict if he felt that it was against the law or the evidence. This important case illuminated the nature of the partnership existing between a judge and jury.

At an earlier time the Supreme Court had held that the words "trial by jury" as used in the Seventh Amendment required a unanimous verdict.[24]

The Court has also held that the word "jury" necessarily involves twelve persons who are reasonably impartial in the case.[25] The Court has reasoned that if there could be fewer than twelve, there is no reason that one would not be enough;

[23] *Capital Traction Co. v. Hof*, 174 U.S. 1, 19 S. Ct. 580 (1899).

[24] *American Publishing Co. v. Fisher*, 166 U.S. 464, 17 S. Ct. 618 (1897); *Springville v. Thomas*, 166 U.S. 707, 17 S. Ct. 717 (1897).

[25] *Thompson v. Utah*, 170 U.S. 343 (1898).

this would destroy the very meaning of the word "jury." Since twelve was the number of people on an English jury when the dual court system was transplanted in America, twelve is the number required by the Seventh Amendment to the Constitution.

To summarize, the Seventh Amendment as interpreted by the Supreme Court provides for a jury comprised of twelve persons, not necessarily men, a unanimous verdict, and a trial in the presence and under the superintendence of a judge empowered to instruct them on the law, to advise them on the facts, and to set aside a verdict if he feels it is against the law or the evidence. Thus, trial by jury in the federal courts preserves the distinction between the judge and the jury, giving the judge the right to expound the law and to apply it in the final analysis, and giving to the jury the right to find the facts and apply them to the law as given by the judge.

Although the Supreme Court has given distinct form to jury trial and meaning to the term "trial by jury," the latter is not and never has been a completely unchanging concept. This is best pointed out by citing two cases.

In *Walker v. Southern Pacific Railroad,*[26] the plaintiff brought an action against the railroad for injuries. The jury returned a general verdict in the plaintiff's favor, but also answered some special questions which were inconsistent with the general verdict. The judge entered judgment for the defendant on these special findings instead of for the plaintiff on the general verdict, and the Supreme Court of the United States affirmed, holding that an act of the legislature changing the form in which a verdict may be rendered and giving primary force to the answers to special questions is not inconsistent with the right of trial by jury. Justice Brewer said:

> . . . *The seventh amendment, indeed, does not attempt to regulate matters of pleading or practice, or to determine in what way issues shall be framed by which questions of fact are to be submitted to a jury.*

[26] 165 U.S. 593, 17 S. Ct. 421 (1897).

Its aim is not to preserve mere matters of form and procedure, but substance of right. This requires that questions of fact in common-law actions shall be settled by a jury, and that the court shall not assume, directly or indirectly, to take from the jury or to itself such prerogative. So long as this substance of right is preserved, the procedure by which this result shall be reached is wholly within the discretion of the legislature, and the courts may not set aside any legislative provision in this respect because the form of action—the mere manner in which questions are submitted—is different from that which obtained at the common law.

Some twenty years later the same Court in *Ex parte Peterson* [27] held that the report of an auditor after examining books could be accepted as valid prima facie evidence of the facts found by him. This did not violate the Seventh Amendment according to Justice Brandeis, who said:

The command of the Seventh Amendment that "the right of trial by jury shall be preserved" does not require that old forms of practice and procedure be retained. . . . It does not prohibit the introduction of new methods for determining what facts are actually in issue, nor does it prohibit the introduction of new rules of evidence. Changes in these may be made. New devices may be used to adapt the ancient institution to present needs and to make it an efficient instrument in the administration of justice. Indeed, such changes are essential to the preservation of the right. The limitation imposed by the Amendments is merely that enjoyment of the right of trial by jury be not obstructed, and that the ultimate determination of issues of fact by the jury be not interfered with.

Later, in *Gasoline Products Co., Inc. v. Champlin Co.* (1931) [28] the Supreme Court in dictum recognized that in

[27] 253 U.S. 300, 40 S. Ct. 543 (1920).
[28] 283 U.S. 494, 51 S. Ct. 513 (1931).

theory a partial new trial would be proper although in the particular case it would not be. Justice Stone pointed out that the Seventh Amendment does not demand the retention of old forms of procedure so as to require a full new trial on all issues when a fair trial has been had on some and not on others which are unrelated.

These and other cases point out a significant feature of the meaning of jury trial: it is not cast in a rigid mold by history. Within the broad framework earlier sketched by the Court, the legislature and the court have to provide improved procedures which will help the jury to function more effectively. On the other hand, the Court will not permit any subversion of the basic concepts of jury trial in the guise of improved procedures.

Judge and jury

As we have seen already in the federal courts, the law-finding function is reserved for the judge, leaving to the jury the fact-finding obligation. Why does the judge exercise this right and determine when cases are to go to the jury? Around the time our Constitution was adopted, there were two methods by which a judge could terminate a trial in which the facts were not sufficient to warrant puzzling over by a jury. These were: (1) ordering an involuntary non-suit, and (2) sustaining a demurrer to the evidence. The first of these was a simple device in which the judge merely ordered the party plaintiff's case to be withdrawn from the judicial arena when he saw that the plaintiff had failed to make his case. In such an instance the plaintiff was permitted to start over with a new lawsuit. The second was a far more complicated procedure, resulting in every instance in a binding judgment either for the plaintiff or for the defendant without a factual trial. As can be seen, each of these had its drawbacks. The first failed to bring the problem to a conclusion, the second brought it to a conclusion in many instances but without a fair determination of the facts.

Before discussing the third and currently most often used method by which this issue is raised, perhaps it would be wise to spell out the problems in simple terms. Let us assume that it is the law of a state that a person who strikes another should respond to that other person in damages for the injuries done, and that the plaintiff contends in a lawsuit that the defendant struck him. The facts, however, merely show that the defendant looked cross-eyed at the plaintiff and there is no evidence of any kind, either from direct testimony or inference, to indicate that the defendant struck or threatened to strike the plaintiff. Of course, it is possible that in such a case a jury could take these facts and in light of the law return a verdict in favor of the defendant. If these facts are true and there is no evidence to indicate otherwise, it is clear that the defendant should not have to respond to the plaintiff in damages. Therefore, why should the jury bother themselves with such a case? Should there not be devised a way whereby such a case can be terminated? The devices of both involuntary non-suit and demurrer to the evidence would permit a termination without the verdict of a jury. This would be permitted on the theory that in taking the evidence to be favorable to the person who has the burden of proof and applying it to the law, there would be no right of the plaintiff to damages.

During the middle of the nineteenth century the difficulties arising from the motions for non-suit and demurrer to the evidence became obvious to a great many lawyers and judges when defendants began requesting in such cases that the jury be instructed to return a verdict in favor of the defendant. They realized that the jury should be told in no uncertain terms that the law was clear and that their verdict must be for the defendant; this was doing no more than the law required. This soon became known as a motion for a directed verdict and raised the question of the status of the law as applied to the facts: was the factual evidence sufficient also to justify a verdict in favor of the plaintiff? If it was, then the case should go to the jury; if not, the case should not go to the jury and the judgment should be entered for the defendant.

With such a procedure questions will obviously arise as to whether or not the court was correct either in submitting a case to the jury or in granting a directed verdict. In the early part of this century the courts used much of their power to shape the law and to take cases from the jury, and the directed verdict was an improved method of doing this. As late as 1939 Justice Black, speaking for the majority of the Supreme Court in *Lyon v. Mutual Benefit Assn.,*[29] specifically held that granting a directed verdict did not in any way deprive a person of his constitutional right to trial by jury. However, less than five years later in *Galloway v. United States,*[30] Justice Black spoke for a dissenting minority urging that the whole process of directing verdicts was contrary to the right of trial by jury and was an encroachment upon a bulwark of civil liberty. He went on to say:

> *. . . Today's decision marks a continuation of a gradual process of judicial erosion which in 150 years has slowly worn away a major portion of the Seventh Amendment. . . .*

The majority of the Court in the *Galloway* case upheld the directed verdict procedure and it remains a valid and effective device for raising questions of law. Justice Black's attack on the directed verdict, however, has had an effect in another way. It has caused the Court to be less likely to grant directed verdicts in cases in which general standards are used in the law, standards of reasonableness, standards of negligence, and so forth. Thus, today we find many more cases being submitted to the good sense and judgment of the jury to decide whether or not these general standards are met.

When the directed verdict first became widely adopted, the test applied before it was used by the courts was whether

29 305 U.S. 484, 59 S. Ct. 297 (1939).
30 319 U.S. 372, 63 S. Ct. 1077 (1943).

there was any evidence in the record to permit the case to go to the jury. If there was such evidence, the case had to go to the jury; if not, a directed verdict could be sustained. This was called the scintilla test. Gradually, through the more liberal granting of directed verdicts, courts changed their focus and permitted judges to decide whether or not they would be required to set a verdict aside as being contrary to the weight of evidence. If they felt that they would be so required, they were to direct a verdict. This has been referred to as the new trial test and gives much more latitude to a trial judge. In recent years, however, particularly in the FELA cases, the Supreme Court has been reversing trial judges who have directed verdicts in almost all cases in which there were general standards to be applied, saying in effect that general standards were for the jury.

Invoking general standards is the community's way of saying that it wants community judgment. The use of general standards in law is an express refusal to be explicit and therefore a denial of the power of the judge to direct a verdict. In *Davis v. Virginian Railway Co.* (1960),[31] the Court emphasized the possibility of fair-minded men reaching different conclusions. In cases where there is a possibility of general standards being involved, the Court said the question should be for the jury to decide. In *Sentilles v. Inter-Caribbean Shipping Corp.* (1959),[32] Justice Brennan quoted an earlier opinion by Justice Murphy:

> . . . *It is not the function of the Court to search the record for conflicting circumstantial evidence in order to take the case away from the jury on a theory that the proof gives equal support to inconsistent and uncertain inferences. The focal point of judicial review is the reasonableness of the particular inference or conclusion drawn by the jury. . . . Courts are not free to reweigh the evidence and set aside the jury verdict merely*

[31] 361 U.S. 354, 80 S. Ct. 387 (1960).
[32] 361 U.S. 107, 80 S. Ct. 137 (1959).

because the jury could have drawn different inferences or conclusions or because judges feel that other results are more reasonable.

In *Baker v. Texas and Pacific Railway Co.* (1959),[33] the Court again emphasized that the "jury's function is to select from among conflicting inferences and conclusions which it considers most reasonable." In *Schulz, Administratrix v. Pennsylvania Railroad Co.* (1956),[34] Justice Black, speaking for the majority of the Court, said:

> . . . *Issues of negligence* * * * *call for the exercise of common sense and sound judgment under the circumstances of the particular case. "[W]e think these are questions for the jury to determine. . . ." Fact finding does not require mathematical certainty. Jurors are supposed to reach their conclusions on the basis of common sense, common understanding and fair beliefs, grounded on evidence consisting of direct statements by witnesses or proof of circumstances from which inferences can fairly be drawn.*

These statements were made in cases involving facts from which many of us would infer no negligence. The Court, however, indicates that it is the function of the jury to make this determination rather than of the courts. The Supreme Court, however, has not permitted a trial judge to abrogate completely his obligation to determine whether or not there is any evidence in the case to go to the jury. In *Inman v. Baltimore and Ohio Railroad Co.* (1959),[35] the Court reversed a verdict in favor of the plaintiff in an FELA case holding that the trial judge had committed an error in not directing a verdict in favor of the defendant since there was no evidence in the case permitting a conclusion to be drawn that the negligence of the employer played any part at all in the injury or death.

[33] 359 U.S. 227, 79 S. Ct. 664 (1959).
[34] 350 U.S. 523, 76 S. Ct. 608 (1956).
[35] 361 U.S. 138, 80 S. Ct. 242 (1959).

Thus the problem today remains the same. A jury trial means a trial before a judge and a jury with the jury passing on the facts only in those cases in which they are sufficient to justify a decision one way or the other, and the judge, in the event that facts are lacking, must make a determination based upon law withdrawing the case from the consideration of the jury. The procedural device used at this point is normally the directed verdict. The issue, however, is a basic issue of law, taking all the established facts into consideration which are favorable to the person having the burden of proof and determining in light of these facts whether the law is sufficiently clear to permit a verdict in favor of that person. The more clear-cut the law is, the more likely are directed verdicts. The more general are the standards to be applied or enunciated in the law, the less likely is it that the court will require directed verdicts.

One of the major drawbacks to the directed verdict procedure is the fact that trial judges are often wrong in their assessment of the sufficiency of the evidence and grant directed verdicts in cases in which a jury should determine the facts. When this is done, the only recourse open to the plaintiff is to appeal to obtain a reversal. If the case is reversed it must go back for a new trial. Thus an error at the initial stage of a trial results in a second trial and a substantial waste of time. More than fifty years ago a group of thoughtful lawyers and judges devised a method whereby this same issue could be held in abeyance until after a trial. Instead of directing a verdict when it was requested, the court was to take the matter under advisement, and upon an appropriate motion after a verdict had been returned in favor of a plaintiff, to determine whether or not there was sufficient evidence to support this verdict. This would permit the whole matter to be determined with one trial only, whether or not the trial judge was correct. If he were correct in granting the motion, the case would be at an end with one trial. If he were incorrect and the Supreme Court reversed him, the case would still be at an end for the verdict would be reinstated.

When a statute of this kind first reached the Supreme Court in the case of *Slocum v. N. Y. Life Ins. Co.*,[36] the Court, in an elaborate and lengthy opinion by Mr. Justice Van Devanter, held that the Seventh Amendment to the Constitution prevented such a procedure from being used. The Court could not set aside a verdict after it had been received and enter a judgment contrary to it, since this would be denying the parties the right to trial by jury. Justice Hughes, speaking for a minority of four, said that it was merely a procedural device carrying forward in point of time the same issue that was raised by the motion for directed verdict, thus making the trial a more simplified, less cumbersome process.

This case stood as the law until 1935 when the Court decided *Baltimore & Carolina Line, Inc. v. Redman*[37] and in effect completely reversed its position in the *Slocum* case. The opinion by the same Justice Van Devanter permitted the parties to reserve the question of law raised by the motion for directed verdict and to consider it by means of a motion for judgment notwithstanding the verdict made at a time subsequent to the verdict. This case permitted a new dimension to be introduced into a lawsuit since it permitted this legal question to be taken up after the verdict and in many instances permitted only one trial rather than two. On the basis of the *Redman* case, the federal rules of civil procedure permitted the automatic reservation of the issue raised by the motion for a directed verdict. However, in *Johnson v. New York, New Haven & Hartford Railroad Co.* (1952),[38] the Court held that failure to make a motion for judgment notwithstanding the verdict at a time subsequent to the verdict would prevent the appellate court from entering a judgment in a case when a verdict should not

[36] 228 U.S. 364, 33 S. Ct. 523 (1913).
[37] 295 U.S. 654, 55 S. Ct. 890 (1935).
[38] 344 U.S. 48, 73 S. Ct. 125 (1952).

have been returned by the jury. In other words, the issue of whether a directed verdict should have been sustained may be raised after the verdict, but it is not automatically raised in the absence of a motion for judgment notwithstanding the verdict.

Thus, the Supreme Court has provided in its rules for a device to test this most important question both before and after the verdict. It is necessary, however, that the motion for directed verdict be made before and after the verdict if it is to be tested, and it is further necessary that a motion for judgment notwithstanding the verdict be made if testing is to occur after the verdict. It is probably not unfair to read into these requirements for strict observance of the rules a feeling of a number of members of the Court that to require less than an absolute observance of the rules would be to erode the right to jury trial.

What kinds of cases?

When the Constitution was adopted, American lawyers were acquainted with the means of trying lawsuits in England. In fact, Blackstone's *Commentaries* provided a judicial bible in this country for many years. In England there were four great courts: the Court of King's Bench, the Court of Common Pleas, the Court of the Exchequer, and the Court of Chancery. As previously pointed out, largely as a result of the refusal of the judges of the Court of the King's Bench to grant relief for a host of wrongs, the king himself had stepped in to aid his subjects, and had permitted his chancellor to grant certain types of relief; this developed more formally into the Court of Chancery. Although the right to jury trial was present in the three original courts, never had it been inherent in the court of the chancellor. At the time the Constitution was adopted, therefore, our forefathers were accustomed to having law cases tried by juries and equity cases tried by the judge. It was not unusual then that this division appeared in the interpretation of the Seventh

Amendment. In 1830 Justice Story traced the theories of the Seventh Amendment in passage and pointed out the distinctions between law and equity.[39]

As long as separate actions had to be commenced for equity relief on the one hand, and law relief on the other, the problems faced by the courts were solved by motions to dismiss actions which were improperly brought. However, in 1938 the federal rules of civil procedure amalgamated actions at law and equity into a common civil action permitting the joinder of equitable and legal claims but reserving the right to jury trial in those cases which were historically law. This has caused a number of problems not easily solved. These were brought to a head in the case of *Beacon Theatres, Inc. v. Westover* (1959),[40] in which Fox Theatres anticipated being sued for treble damages by Beacon Theatres for an antitrust violation. They sought a declaratory judgment which would have settled some of the key issues in the damage action and asked that Beacon's suit be temporarily enjoined. Upon being sued for a declaratory judgment, Beacon filed a counterclaim, raising issues which would have come up in its suit for treble damages. It also demanded a jury trial. The district judge, purporting to exercise discretion under the federal rules of civil procedure, ruled that he would try the issues common to both proceedings as an equity case without a jury before proceeding with Beacon's counterclaim which would be tried by a jury. On an appeal to the Supreme Court, it was decided that the district court had to set aside its ruling, for it had denied Beacon the right to jury trial. Although the issues involved in the case were common to the suit for treble damages (the law issues) and to the request for the injunction (the equity issue), the Supreme Court said that to do less than give Beacon a trial by jury on these issues would be to deny its right to a jury trial under the Seventh Amendment. If Beacon

39 *Parsons v. Bedford,* 28 U.S. 433 (1830).
40 359 U.S. 500, 79 S. Ct. 948 (1959).

had been entitled to a jury trial in the treble damage suit it could not be deprived of that right merely because an injunction action was filed first.

There was strong dissent in this case, alleging that this interpretation of the federal rules undermined the basic structure of equity jurisprudence which had been developed over centuries and was explicitly recognized by the Constitution. It was the feeling of the dissenting judges that this case carried the right to jury trial far beyond the place it would naturally have had if there had been no declaratory judgment act or amalgamation of law and equity procedure in the federal rules. At any rate, it seems clear that from the time this case was decided the power of a judge to decide facts in equitable issues has been taken away from him when these issues are consolidated with law issues based on the same facts. The Supreme Court has gone far in solving the law-equity problem by insisting on the superiority of the claim to a jury trial in situations involving questions germane to both.

Federal jury and state law

State law determines the rights of parties in cases in the federal courts only because of the diversity of citizenship of the plaintiffs and the defendants. The question now arises as to whether or not state law will determine the right to jury trial or whether courts will look to federal standards. Two recent cases have bearing upon this question. In the case of *Byrd v. Blue Ridge Rural Electric Cooperative, Inc.* (1958),[41] the plaintiff in a diversity case claimed a right to jury trial under the federal law, while the defendant claimed that actions arising under the South Carolina's Workmen's Compensation Act, which he asserted provided the exclusive remedy, were to be tried without a

[41] 356 U.S. 525, 78 S. Ct. 893 (1958).

jury. The Court held that even though state decisions specify that this issue be tried without a jury, the plaintiff is entitled in the federal court to have the factual issues presented to a jury. In the first place, the state rule requiring judicial determination was not so bound up with the state-created rights and obligations as to require a non-jury trial in the federal courts, and second, there is a strong policy against allowing the state rules to disrupt the judge-jury relationship in the federal courts under the Seventh Amendment. The function assigned to the jury is essential in the trial process and is protected by the Constitution. This case seems to imply that the federal jury right may not be impeded by a different state method for deciding facts unless a state-created right is so much involved in the procedure for trial that it cannot be separated from it.

This view was again expressed in the case of *Magenau, Administrator v. Aetna Freight Lines, Inc.* (1959).[42] In this case the petitioner sought to recover damages for the wrongful death of the decedent who was killed when a tractor-trailer leased by the respondent crashed off a Pennsylvania highway. The case was tried in the federal district court on the basis of diversity citizenship jurisdiction. A jury returned a verdict for the petitioner on a negligence theory but the court of appeals reversed it, maintaining that, since the decedent was the respondent's employee, the Pennsylvania Workmen's Compensation Act provided the exclusive remedy. On appeal to the Supreme Court it was held that the question of employment should have been decided by the jury regardless of the practice in the state court. Following the *Byrd* case, Justice Clark said that this type of question must go to the jury unless the state practice of assigning such factual issues to the judge has been "announced as an integral part of the special relationship created by the statute." These recent cases are but a part of

[42] 360 U.S. 273, 79 S. Ct. 1184 (1959).

the fortress that the Supreme Court is building around the right to trial by jury.

THE JURY IN THE STATES

Federal Constitutional provisions

The Constitutional provisions for right of trial by jury previously referred to apply only in the federal courts. On several occasions the Supreme Court has held that nothing in the Constitution requires a state to provide a right to trial by jury in civil cases and has sustained means of trial other than by jury as meeting due process of law. This it did in a case permitting a judge to decide a case when the jury could not reach a verdict,[43] in a workmen's compensation case heard before a workmen's compensation board instead of a jury,[44] in a case tried under a state statute creating a certain lien on land and not providing for trial by jury,[45] in a mandamus case,[46] in quo warranto proceedings,[47] in an eminent domain proceeding tried before a commission,[48] and in a suit to try title.[49]

State constitutions

As has already been indicated, the constitutions of almost all the states contain provisions somewhat similar to those found in the federal Constitution, guaranteeing the right to trial by jury in civil cases. Although the interpretation of these provisions may differ from those of the federal Constitution, there is a strong tendency on the part of each of the states to protect carefully the right to jury trial. The differences, however, should be pointed out.

[43] *Walker v. Sauvinet,* 92 U.S. 90 (1875).
[44] *N. Y. Central R. R. Co. v. White,* 243 U.S. 188, 37 S. Ct. 247 (1917).
[45] *Marvin v. Trout,* 199 U.S. 212, 26 S. Ct. 31 (1905).
[46] *In re Delgado,* 140 U.S. 586, 11 S. Ct. 874 (1891).
[47] *Wilson v. North Carolina,* 169 U.S. 586, 18 S. Ct. 435 (1898).
[48] *Long Island Water Supply Co. v. Brooklyn,* 166 U.S. 685, 17 S. Ct. 718 (1897).
[49] *Church v. Kelsey,* 121 U.S. 282, 7 S. Ct. 897 (1887).

1. A number of states permit a verdict to be less than unanimous, sometimes by eight, nine, or ten jurors.

2. Some states provide for juries of less than twelve.

3. Some states have not been as restrictive as was the Supreme Court in the case of *Beacon Theatres, Inc. v. Westover,*[50] when it required that issues common to law and equity in a single case must be decided by a jury.

4. A number of states do not require a motion for directed verdict before an effective motion for judgment notwithstanding the verdict is made after a verdict has been returned.

In most instances, however, these are procedural differences and do not involve the fundamental right of trial by jury. The right seems to be as well protected in the states as in the federal courts.

IN OTHER COUNTRIES

In most other civilized countries civil disputes are resolved by referring them to a judge or a panel of judges. Even in England the jury has virtually disappeared as a means of resolving civil disputes. Sir Patrick Devlin reports:[51]

> *In civil litigation there has been in the last century a marked decline not only in the popularity of trial by jury but also in the facilities that are afforded for it. Until 1854, trial by jury was the only form of trial used in any court of common law. In that year the first small breach was made. Trial by a judge alone could thereafter be had by consent of both parties and the judge was empowered to refer matters of account. The next change was made in 1873, the great year of law reform; the power to remit matters of account to a referee was extended to "matters requiring prolonged*

50 *Supra,* n. 40.
51 Devlin, TRIAL BY JURY, pp. 130–133 (1956).

examination of documents or accounts or any scientific or local investigation"; this phraseology is still part of the law. A more significant though subtler change was made in 1883. Six causes of action were selected for special treatment and, with one addition made later, they are still placed in a separate category; they are libel, slander, malicious prosecution, false imprisonment, seduction, and breach of promise of marriage. In these six cases trial by jury continued to be obtainable as a matter of course, but in all other cases it had to be specially asked for. Thus, while the right to a jury was maintained in all cases except those in the "prolonged examination" class, the alteration was so contrived as to make trial by a judge alone appear to be the general rule and trial by jury the exception. Later, the procedure was tightened by requiring the application for a jury to be made within a fixed time limit.

The war of 1914–1918 provided a good ground for at least a temporary change, for towards the end of it jurors were no longer easily available. In 1918 the right to a jury was abolished except in seven cases, viz., *the six cases previously enumerated together with cases of fraud; in all other cases trial by jury was made discretionary. The Act of 1918 was a piece of emergency legislation designed to expire six months after the end of the war, but when it did expire, it was replaced by another Act intended to be permanent. As a permanent alteration it was not well received; indeed, it was criticized so severely that in 1925 Parliament restored the* status quo ante *1918. But the restoration was not long lived. In 1933, as part of a drive for cheaper litigation, Parliament substantially re-enacted the 1920 Act, the chief alteration being that the right to a jury in cases of fraud was granted only to the party charged. This is the present position. As it has lasted now for twenty-three years and has been accompanied by an immense decline in the volume of trials by juries, one must take it as settled.*

Up to 1913 there was still trial by jury in the majority of cases; the figures show that in that year there was a jury of 55 per cent. of the cases tried in the High Court. By 1918 that figure was reduced to 36 per cent.; and in 1919, the first year when the new legislation took full effect, it was down to 16½ per cent. Then came the post-war litigation boom, remembrances of which can still give elderly barristers a severe attack of nostalgia. The desire of litigants to get their cases on and have them expeditiously tried was a powerful aid to the new legislation. In 1920, 1921 and 1922 the number of cases tried in one or the other form was nearly two and a half times as great as in 1913 and the proportion of jury trials had fallen to 10 per cent. or below; in 1922 it was nearly down to 8 per cent. Thereafter, as the volume of litigation fell, the proportion increased; and when by 1926 the legislative status quo *was restored, the figure was up to over 36 per cent. and remained at about that level until after 1933. After the new enactment of that year it fell fairly sharply (in 1935 it was down to 12 per cent.) and the war of 1939–45 completed the debacle.*

The popularity of trial by judge alone is now decisively established; the proportion of jury trials is now 2 per cent. or 3 per cent. of the whole. About half of this is composed of the excepted cases (which form only a minute fraction of civil litigation) and the other half consists of cases in which a successful application has been made by one side or the other—usually a plaintiff and often with a case that is weak in law.

It must not be supposed that this severe decline is

due to a jury being refused when asked for; the number of refusals is in fact quite negligible. An attempt after 1933 to suggest that trial by jury ought not to be granted unless there was a special reason for it was decisively negatived by the full Court of Appeal, which held that the discretion to grant it was quite unfettered. The decline is due to the fact that juries are not being asked for. One of the causes of that is undoubtedly the decline itself which made trial by jury an exceptional proceeding: there is a strong tendency on the part of practitioners—particularly solicitors' managing clerks —to avoid exceptional procedure and to stick to the paths with which they are familiar. The sort of cases in which it is applied for are those where personal issues are involved, e.g., *an allegation of misconduct and wrongful dismissal or a quarrel leading to an assault. Cases within the excepted classes are not invariably trial by jury. Cases of libel and slander, for example, are quite frequently submitted by the parties to a judge alone and a defendant charged with fraud prefers, more often than not, not to claim his right to a jury.*

This revolution in the mode of trial in England should not be construed as an indictment of the use of the civil jury in America. Great differences exist between that country and this in many matters, not the least of which is the method of selecting judges. Here, judges are usually popularly elected. Any lawyer who is able to convince the electorate that he should be a judge will become a judge, whereas in England judges are appointed from among the best lawyers of the bar. In this country judges generally serve for short terms, necessarily having to think about running for re-election and in many instances spending much time in becoming re-elected, whereas in England judges are appointed for life.

The decline in the use of the civil jury in England has

developed over a period of more than 50 years as a result of a gradual erosion. Little by little the right has been whittled away until it is now almost all gone. This should give us pause in this country.

We know that other countries do not use the jury in dispute resolution, and that we need not try to export our institutions to improve their judicial systems, nor import theirs and believe it to be superior to ours. We must direct our attention to what we have in the jury system, to a determination of whether it is sound, and, if it isn't, to how it can be improved. The institution which we employ to resolve disputes must be tested against facts and conditions prevailing in *this* country, not in others.

III

BASIC STRENGTHS OF THE CIVIL JURY

In the preceding chapters I have attempted to place in perspective the jury's role in deciding facts in the adjudicative process, to explain the operation of that process, to compare the various methods of resolving disputes, to describe the differences between the judge and the jury and the reasons for the functions of each, to point out some of the fundamental ideas involved in dispute resolution and the place that the fact-finder plays, and to state briefly the history and development of the civil jury and its present place in constitutional law. At this point I should like briefly to summarize some of the reasons already mentioned why the civil jury has attained such a strong position in our system of dispute resolution.

ACCEPTANCE BY THE PUBLIC

Decisions by juries seem to have been accorded wide public acceptance in this country. I am sure that fewer jury decisions are criticized by the public than are decisions by judges. We must always remember that law ultimately derives its support from the public and that, although law is in many instances far removed from the people, public acceptance of the operation of our legal system is still important. Perhaps the best demonstration of public acceptance of jury trials is given by Professor Kalven of the Chicago Jury Project. He reported that 70 per cent of the public favored jury trial while only 9 per cent favored trial by the judge. Recently, when those who had participated in jury service were polled, the percentage favoring jury trials was 77 per cent.[52]

APPLICATION OF GENERAL STANDARDS

The laws by which all of us live are not series of hard and fast rules but, on the whole, a number of general statements full of ambiguities, full of "reasonableness," and so on. These general standards must be interpreted in individual cases in a way that is understood by the community, otherwise, it will not live by them. The very purpose of using general language is to permit interpretation by the community from which the jury is chosen and of which it supposedly represents a cross section. The jury is probably not an unfair way to obtain a sense of that community in interpreting these general standards. A judge is much less a representative of the cross section of the community. He is normally selected from the elite, and gifted in a great many ways, but not necessarily capable of sensing broad community standards. If it were possible to reduce all law to black and white distinctions, it would then be possible to eliminate judges and juries, substituting machines to do the work of courts. Such law, however, would probably do far more injustice than justice since we, as fallible beings, would never be able to conceive of all the problems faced by people, let alone to solve them and translate the solutions into legal language. If this were done, there wouldn't be enough books in which to print all the law; no one could know it all. We must then continue to use general principles and standards, allowing for some community interpretation.

[52] Kalven, "Report on the Chicago Jury Project," AIMS AND METHODS OF LEGAL RESEARCH, (1955).

BACKGROUND PREJUDICE AND PREJUDGING OF FACTS

Everybody, of course, carries with him a certain number of prejudices and biases, some strong and some weak. Jurors are not exempt from them, nor are judges. In one respect, however, jurors bring fewer prejudices to the decision-making process than do judges, for it is well known that a person who does the same thing day after day, year after year, becomes biased about that thing. A judge who sits day after day hearing automobile accident cases may become prejudiced in some way about these cases. Some judges may be pro-plaintiff, others pro-defendant. The juror, on the other hand, is nonprofessional. He does not hear a series of similar cases each day; he hears only one, or at most, a few. Because he hears so few he is interested and pays attention. He does not say, "Oh, this is just like the one I had the day before yesterday"; he attempts to judge the facts. In this respect, I think, the juror has fewer prejudices than the judge. As far as over-all prejudices are concerned, I suppose the two may be about the same, but the deliberative process of decision in the jury room has been established as a means of rendering somewhat neutral these over-all prejudices. The decisions of groups after deliberation show far fewer prejudices than do the decisions of individuals. Because the prejudices tend to disappear in jury decisions due to exposure to criticism on the part of other jurors, the process of deliberation leading to jury decisions is so significant that it is perhaps the basic strength of the civil jury.

CITIZEN PARTICIPATION IN GOVERNMENT AT THE NONPROFESSIONAL LEVEL

It has been reported that more than one million citizens serve on juries each year, a significant portion of our population. Because of the jury a great many people are involved in responsible governmental decision-making who probably never before and perhaps never again may become so involved in it. Such a popular appreciation of the difficulty of governmental decision-making is unless they have been involved in it. Such a popular appreciation of the difficulty of decision-making by government officials will go a long way toward supporting democratic government. More than any other single institution, the jury has brought people into government. It has brought them in as amateurs, has permitted them to serve for a short period, and has returned them to society more experienced in the problems of responsible decision-making. This valuable education in government cannot be underestimated as a significant strength of the civil jury.

UNDUE EXPANSION OF THE BUREAUCRACY OF DECISION-MAKING

As has been pointed out, the American people have been somewhat opposed to big government in the past. This opposition has lessened to permit our present big government. Only at the local level do we have significant citizen participation in government, and jury service provides the greatest opportunity for that participation. If all of the tasks which juries now perform were to be undertaken by judges or commissioners, and if the same quality of justice now obtained through jury deliberation were to be retained, it would be necessary to supplement greatly the number of judges, both at the trial level and at the appellate level. Besides judges, additional clerks, reporters, and court staff would have to be employed. Whether this would ever develop into a bureaucracy of decision-making may be questioned, but the use of the jury lessens the chance of this happening.

CHECKS AND BALANCES

Trial by jury involves a trial before a judge and jury, the jury consisting of twelve reasonably impartial people, and a unanimous verdict under instructions from the judge who has the power to set aside a verdict if it is erroneous. This is the traditional and Constitutional concept of jury trial, involving a series of checks and balances which have been devised to obtain justice for litigants in the final judgment entered by the court. In no other method of trial are these checks and balances so carefully developed: the jury checks the judge and finds the facts, which are then applied to the law given by the judge, thereby allowing a composite verdict to be reported; by the same token the judge checks the jury, rules upon the evidence to be presented, instructs the jury on the law, and enters the judgment based upon the verdict, which he can set aside if it is erroneous. Lawyers assist the judge and the jury, providing the law for the judge, stating the claims of the parties, and producing the facts, evidence, and proof for the jury.

Arbitrariness on the part of any one of these three agents can easily be corrected and bias on the part of any can easily be stamped out. These checks and balances work so well that the final check of the judge on the jury, the granting of a new trial, is seldom exercised.

If we look at a trial before a judge alone, we find that many of the checks and balances are missing. The judge decides the law and finds the facts, enters the judgment, and checks himself. The only check upon the judge comes from the lawyers who, in this trial as well, produce the law and the facts and make the claims upon which the judgment is based.

IV

A CRITIQUE OF THE JURY SYSTEM

The civil jury is not without its critics. A great many thoughtful people have urged that it be abolished either in whole or in certain prescribed instances. Their writings are of sufficient importance that an objective study of the civil jury should fully state and examine these criticisms to determine whether they have merit.

In examining them four questions must be asked:

1. Is the assertion true? Is the criticism valid? If not, it must then be rejected.

2. If the criticism is valid, does it apply equally well to other modes of trial? If so, then it is an indictment not of the jury but of the trial process itself, and should not be used in any way to condemn the jury.

3. Are the critical points inherent in the jury system or do they involve only some non-fundamental part of the jury system that can be corrected? It would be a shame to destroy a system which had proved to be of such value merely because one or more corrections were not made.

4. If we find that there are valid criticisms directed only at the jury that cannot be corrected in any way, we must weigh the damage done by these shortcomings against the positive features of the civil jury.

Each of these questions must be asked and answered with respect to the following points of criticism.

ARBITRARINESS

We constantly hear that the jury is arbitrary, unpredictable, and subject to passion. Each of us within our own experience can probably find a verdict of a jury which is difficult to explain. It is not unlikely that juries on occasion are arbitrary, unpredictable, and subject to passion. To deny it would be to deny a well established fact. But, do not decisions by judges in the absence of juries sometimes appear to exhibit these same qualities? Any lawyer can probably point out as many cases in which this criticism can be made of judges as well as juries. It seems doubtful that any dispute-resolving process could be developed that would not be abused at some time or another by arbitrariness, unpredictability, or passion. We do not yet have machines into which we can feed information and from which perfect verdicts are ejected. I am sure that if we had such machines the difficulty of stating our legal standards of conduct to anticipate all circumstances would prevent us from using them.

The psychological studies previously reported and the reports of the Chicago Jury Project indicate that there is no more significant variation in the decisions of juries on similar facts than there is in the decision of judges. This criticism then, although it may be a valid one, seems to be inherent in the decision-making process rather than solely a criticism of the jury.

Our present method of trial by jury is a fine balance between the obligations of the jury on the one hand and the judge on the other. Each is involved in the total process of resolving the dispute. The checks and balances built into our method of trial, involving both the judge and the jury, tend to eliminate from the final result the arbitrariness that sometimes creeps into the decisions of one or the other of its parts.

COURT CONGESTION

It is asserted by a vociferous and persistent group of people that the jury trial creates court congestion. This is true, it is argued, because it takes some time to select a jury, because lawyers spend more time trying a case before a jury, and because it takes some time to instruct the jury and for the jury to deliberate. All of this, it is asserted, is time spent over and above that which would be taken by a trial before a judge. Therefore, when cases pile up on the docket, it is argued that the additional time taken by jury trials is a significant aggravation of this congestion, particularly in a number of our metropolitan areas. This criticism should be studied in two ways. First, a step-by-step analysis of the trial process itself should be undertaken to determine whether or not more time is taken by a jury trial than by a trial by judge; second, an examination should be made of any studies that might throw light on the matter.

These studies would reveal the following to be true. When a case is tried before a judge, it does not proceed with the same dispatch as if it were tried before a jury. When a jury is drawn and sworn, it is kept together until the case is settled, whereas this is not the case in a trial before a judge, who may interrupt the case to hear other matters. Lawyers know that when they start a case before a jury they must have their witnesses and evidence ready. If they do not, they may have to do without them. When a case is tried before a judge, however, the lawyer for one side may be ready to produce some evidence while the lawyer for the other side may ask for a continuance of the case. Six months later they may come back and produce some more evidence. They may go back and forth in this manner, taking a very long time indeed to resolve a specific case. Although Dickens' *Bleak House* may somewhat overstate the problems of judge trials today, the problems remain and to a lesser degree the same criticisms can be made of them. In many parts of the country trials by judge drag on interminably. Continuance after continuance causes trials to last for long periods of time, and this starting and stopping of the case tends to prevent the full focus of the judge on the issues of the case. On the other hand, once a jury is impaneled the trial goes quickly to completion, usually without continuances since the twelve jurors cannot be made to interrupt their normal lives for the length of time that a trial with continuances would take.

It is also unfair to assume that trial by judge is over after the evidence has been presented, when a jury requires instructions and deliberation. Judges also have to deliberate and instruct themselves on the law. Findings of fact and law must be prepared by the judge and he must be satisfied with them. Judges may sit on cases for months before deciding them and, although they can be working on other matters during this time, the cases still drag on and on, causing court congestion. The point of this is not to condemn judges who, on the whole, are doing a good job, but to put in perspective some of the fallacious comparisons made by others of the two modes of trial.

Objective analysis of the two methods of trying cases, then, does not lead inevitably to the conclusion that more cases can be tried before judges than before juries and that therefore court congestion is caused by jury trials.

Let us look at what others have said about this matter. A short time ago, as part of the Chicago jury study, the researchers Zeisel, Kalven, and Buchholz attempted to find the chief cause of the delay in the courts. (A portion of this study appears later on in this book.) They found that although it takes a little longer to try a case before a jury than a case before a judge in New York City, it does not take much longer. It does not take much longer to try a case before a judge in New York City than it takes to try a similar case in New Jersey. When one takes into consideration a factor not considered by these researchers—the time it takes a judge to deliberate and write his opinion—the time difference between a jury trial and a judge trial is very little indeed. In fact, the jury trial may be the shorter of the two. Whichever is less time consuming, the difference is negligible, particularly when one considers the advantages of the jury trial. Certainly the results of the Chicago study should controvert any serious contention that delay is inherent in the jury system.

EXPENSE

It is argued that the jury is an expensive luxury. The fact that it does cost money has validity because all twelve jurors must be paid for their time of duty, even though I do not think they are paid enough. The state does not pay for the loss of time from their jobs, it pays them only a nominal salary to do their duty in coming forward to serve their government.

In considering the problem of expense we should start with the premise that under no circumstances would we want a single person deciding all cases. The element of deliberation is so significant in the decision-making process that we should not want to turn over all fact-finding to a single judge. If we were to retain the element of deliberation in this fact-finding process without a jury, it would be necessary to have, as do a number of foreign countries, a panel of three or more judges. This would retain the deliberative element and many of the attributes of the jury system. A comparison of the cost of the jury system and the three-judge system (necessitating three times as many judges as there are at present), however, would show that the jury's expense is not greater and may be in fact substantially less. Whether these additional judges would be called judges or commissioners, as has been suggested, would make no difference since the number of new judges would have to be the same and the salaries of commissioners would surely not be less than those of the judges.

There is some doubt, however, whether such a court would eliminate the prejudices that are eliminated in the deliberation of non-professional jurors, since a great deal of bias would arise from the judges doing and hearing the same kind of thing constantly, as has been mentioned earlier.

If professionals were used instead of jurors, lost would be a great deal of citizen participation in government that takes place through the jury, and governmental hierarchy would be expanded.

Even if there were only one judge, the cost of litigation would probably be increased because appeals are filed almost as a matter of course, adding substantially to the total cost of cases. It has been true in equity cases that when a single judge decides facts a rather broad right of appeal on them is desired. A broad appeal on fact in this situation is necessary to check the arbitrariness of a non-deliberative decision, for there can be no deliberation in single-judge courts. The trial process in such a court would work something like this: the trial itself is a preliminary step leading to an ultimate decision, during which the evidence is presented and a preliminary finding made by the judge. In almost every case an appeal is filed as a matter of course to obtain the ultimate decision from a higher court. This not only involves a single judge at the lower level but a multitude of judges at the higher level, thus greatly increasing the cost and the time involved in litigation. This is one of the reasons why present equity practice is so expensive.

To summarize then, if we desired to do away with the jury and at the same time to retain the same quality of justice as is provided by the jury, it would be necessary to provide three or more judges at the trial level or a type of automatic appeal to a higher court. But both of these would tend to increase the cost of trying lawsuits, perhaps to a greater extent than the jury does now.

TECHNICAL EVIDENCE

It has been asserted that the jury is the reason for the development of technical rules of evidence. It is true, I am sure, that evidence rules developed partly because of the jury, although they are now used in all forms of trial, whether or not before a jury. Throughout the country tribunals deciding all kinds of matters are using basically the same evidence rules, and all of the codes of evidence that are being proposed to relax the evidence rules and lessen technical evidential difficulties apply equally as much to judge trials as to jury trials. There is very little proof that evidence presented to a jury is significantly different from evidence presented to a judge or that the time taken to present evidence to each varies greatly.

It is untrue, however, that the jury is to blame for the technicalities arising from the rules of evidence. These technicalities have resulted from the proliferations of judicial decisions involving evidence, a great many of which have come out of judge trials as well as jury trials. Judicial decisions develop and state rules of evidence which are then followed in subsequent decisions. Gradually more and more technicalities are introduced. At present the law of evidence is admittedly technical and burdensome, but jury trials are not to blame.

EXCESSIVE ERRORS

It has been stated that excessive errors occur during jury trials. I have neither seen nor heard anything to substantiate this statement. If there is a problem, it is not one of creating excessive errors; more likely it lies in the area of the difficulty of correcting errors which occur in the jury system. Here we have a real problem, since it is more difficult, of course, to correct an error in a jury trial than in a judge trial. In the judge trial, errors are corrected by a type of equity appeal, sometimes resulting in a final determination of all matters in the case by an appellate court. In the jury trial, on the other hand, errors can be corrected only by reversing the case and sending it back for a new trial because the parties to the case have a right to jury trial on questions of fact. This increases the expense and extends the time of trial, and is something that people who desire to save trial by jury must face. On the other hand, a judge trial must provide a broad right of appeal on the facts if there is to be the element of deliberation in the decisional process. This means more appeals in trials before single judges, making the expense of such a trial perhaps equally as great or greater than the expense of a jury trial.

V

METHODS OF STRENGTHENING THE JURY

BETTER ORIGINAL SELECTION, SCREENING, AND USE OF JURORS

More than 20 years ago a Committee on Trial by Jury of the Section of Judicial Administration of the American Bar Association recognized that serious charges were being leveled at jury trials: "lawyers and judges must face the fact that the system of jury trials is undergoing criticism in many jurisdictions. These criticisms are varied in nature but most of them could be eliminated by proper selection of jurors in the first instance, by courageous refusal on the part of the bench to accept inadequate excuses for not serving as jurors, and, by proper conduct of jury trials by the bar and bench, together with proper quartering, protection, and instruction to jurors. Jury service today is the chief remaining governmental function in which lay citizens take a direct and active part, and trial by jury is the best means within our knowledge of keeping the administration of justice in tune with the community. It is highly important that everything be done which can be done to insure the most efficient method of jury selection and trial procedure." [53]

This thoughtful Committee recognized that quality was important in judicial fact-finding and that the careful selec-

[53] Committee on Trial by Jury, Section of Judicial Administration, American Bar Association (1942).

tion of those who would find facts as jurors would remove much of the criticism that has been directed at the trial jury. If the system of jury trials is to continue, if laymen are to continue to be involved in government as jurors, we must be certain that those who serve on juries have a capacity to think and to understand problems.

We should also make every effort to see that we do not have on the juries all women, or unemployed persons, or old men, or all of any other homogeneous group. We must have a reasonably fair cross section of the community if the jury is to reflect community concern for problems and if the administration of justice is to be kept in tune with the community. We have already seen how important it is to have community involvement in decision-making when general standards are used, and we have asserted that the jury is a better way to accomplish this than having the decision made by a single judge. If the jury does not represent a reasonably fair cross section of the community, there is no community involvement. Therefore, it is important to insure that it does.

Unfortunately, this has not been accomplished in all of our states and localities today. In Michigan, for example, there are a great many ways to obtain jurors for the jury panel and only in some of its localities is a fair cross section of the community obtained. This can best be achieved by using what is called a key-number system for drawing jurors, involving the arbitrary selection of every *nth* name on a voting list. The voting list is used because it includes probably the most complete cross section of the reasonably intelligent people of the community, and if every *nth* name is drawn, the laws of chance should see to it that there are some women and some men, rich and poor, intelligent and not so intelligent, constituting a panel that should represent the approximate ratio of the numbers in each of these groups to the members of the community as a whole.

Having selected a panel in this way, a second need arises for a more adequate screening of the members of the panel. At the present time this screening is accomplished by a series of questions asked of the jury by the lawyers or the judge in a particular case. This is time consuming and sometimes not very revealing. Lawyers often use this *voir dire* examination to indoctrinate jurors in their theory of the case by asking questions which plant ideas in jurors' minds. This questioning could be much more effective if, before a trial, other facts not obviously pertaining to it were disclosed by means of a written questionnaire. With such a device, questions of significance to the lawyers could be asked that could not, in good conscience, be asked in open court. These questionnaires, when made available to the lawyers, would enable them to exercise their challenges more effectively, and those jurors who were not fit for a particular case by reason of personal bias, conscious or unconscious, could be excused.[54] This procedure would shorten the *voir dire* examination.

A third problem which prevents the most effective use of the jury involves the length of time that jurors are asked to serve and the kinds of accommodations that are made available for them. At the present time in a great many parts of the country, almost anyone who desires to be excused from jury duty can concoct a reasonable excuse to obtain his release. Since people who are daily earning more money at their regular jobs than the nominal per diem amount paid jury members are most apt to ask to be excused, the jury panel in most instances is left with women, or men who are either unemployed or too old to work. These people do not represent a fair cross section of the community. The difficulty arises from the fact that we have not brought home

[54] For examples of the type of questionnaire, see Rule 510, COURT RULES, PART III REPORT OF THE JOINT COMMITTEE ON MICHIGAN PROCEDURAL REVISION (1960).

to our people the importance of the obligation of citizens to serve on juries, and we have not made it easy for them to serve by shortening the term of service. Instead of requiring service for three months as is often the case today, why could we not require service for a period not in excess of two weeks. If this were the case, a judge could say without compunction to each person who is chosen: "Mr. Blank, we are sorry that you think that you must be excused; we feel, however, that this is an obligation you must fulfill and we hope that this year you will give up your vacation for this service. You will be required to serve." Legitimate excuses would excuse the juror only for a period of time and he would be required to serve the short two-week term at some later time. A list of dates might be made available from which the prospective juror could select the one most convenient for him. A short term would encourage the service of those who now give excuses and would create a jury that is a reasonably fair cross section of the community.

Sad as it may seem, jurors in a great many cities presently are often kept waiting for hours on end, uninformed as to what is going on in the courtroom. This could be corrected by the thoughtful judge in a great many ways. While this necessary waiting process goes on, better facilities could be made available to the jury. If businessmen could have a telephone, typewriter, desk, and dictation equipment, much of the hardship arising from jury service could be eliminated, since their business activity could be carried on while they were waiting to serve. Thoughtfulness toward those who must serve with inadequate compensation would encourage jury service and discourage applications for release from its rigorous duties.

Conclusion. All states should adopt a key-number system or other random method of choosing jurors and adequate screening questionnaires should be used on every jury panel. Short jury terms should be provided, and no excuses should be allowed because of the short term. Comfortable facilities, including a desk, telephone, dictating equipment, and typewriter should be furnished jurors during a waiting period to lessen the hardship of jury service.

PRE-TRIAL CONFERENCE

In most cases decided by jury, the jury is instructed by the court on a series of issues that must be resolved factually or legally. In many instances these issues are somewhat spurious since the lawyers and the judge, not having carefully screened prospective issues at the beginning of the case, now arrive at the time for the jury to deliberate on its verdict. Issues are submitted to the jury that were thought to be relevant when the case began, regardless of the real facts and issues which were revealed during the trial. Within the past thirty years a way has been found to alleviate this problem substantially. Before the trial a great many courts conduct what is called a pre-trial conference. One of the principal purposes of this conference is to simplify the issues for trial. The judge inquires deeply into the real problems of the case and after this inquiry dictates a memorandum which forms the basis of the trial and indicates the issues to be tried. Such a conference has proved to be so successful in simplifying issues, shortening trials, and making jury deliberations more meaningful that its use is spreading rapidly throughout the country. A simplification of the issues prior to trial usually means more careful preparation and presentation of the lawyers' cases to the jury in the light of these issues, more effective deliberation on the part of the jury, less tangential thinking, and probably a verdict that more accords with what is actually involved in the case because of better understanding of the law as it pertains to these issues. Such pre-trial conferences are valuable whether the matter is decided by a judge or by a jury.

However, for a jury that has to be instructed on the law such simplification of the issues is of paramount importance.

Conclusion. All states should use a pre-trial conference to simplify issues for trial and for submission to the jury.

LESS THAN UNANIMOUS VERDICT

Only a very small percentage of juries are unable to agree on a verdict and therefore "hang." This is often caused when one juror, for one reason or another, is different from the rest and refuses to agree. Deliberation has occurred, biases have been worked out, false premises have been exposed, and yet one juror has not been swayed to the prevailing opinion.

Deliberation so essential to good decision-making and fact-finding does not require unanimity. However, it does require more than a majority verdict, for the give-and-take of discussion is essential. Certainly a verdict requiring ten votes would result in as much deliberation as would a verdict requiring twelve. If only ten votes were necessary, one or two peculiar jurors could not hang a jury, yet the verdict rendered by the ten would in all probability involve as much deliberation as would the normal verdict rendered by twelve.

Conclusion. A ten-vote verdict should be adopted since it would involve as much deliberation as a unanimous one, at the same time preventing one or two people who cannot agree with the others from hanging a jury and making necessary a whole new trial.[55]

IS THE NUMBER "TWELVE" MAGIC?

Almost all states require twelve jurors. The number twelve came into our law as a result of an accident. It is a

[55] This might involve a constitutional amendment in view of the Supreme Court's view in *American Publishing Co. v. Fisher, supra,* n. 24.

good number, sufficient to promote deliberation and to obtain a fair cross section of the community. However, there is no evidence to show that deliberation requires twelve people. In fact, it could easily be argued that a six-man jury would deliberate equally as well as one of twelve and that five out of the six ought to be able to reach a verdict with as much deliberation as ten out of twelve. A six-man jury at the same time would be less expensive, would save time in the selection of a jury, and very likely would provide sufficient deliberation and a community cross section. The constitutional right of trial by a jury of twelve could be preserved by granting the right to demand a jury of twelve. If that demand were made, the party demanding it would be required to pay the full cost of the jury, including their salaries, and this payment would not be taxable as costs in the case. In such a case it is very likely that the parties would go ahead with a jury of six, and that gradually all juries would be reduced to six people.

Conclusion. States should consider using juries of six.

INSTRUCTING THE JURY

One of the weaknesses of jury decision-making lies in the instructions on the law given the jury at the close of a case. The verdict the jury renders in a civil case is normally a combination of fact and law. "We, the jury, find in favor of the plaintiff and assess damages at $——," or "We, the jury, find in favor of the defendant." To render such a verdict the jury must not only hear the facts but must also be instructed in the legal propositions applicable to the case. On the whole, judges have done a very poor job of instructing. Some of them ramble on interminably, using legal language not easily understood by the jury, which not uncommonly fails to grasp some significant question of law as a result. If better verdicts are to be had, attention must be given to the instructional process.

Care should be exercised to draft instructions in laymen's

language. In a number of states, easily understood standard jury instructions are already being adopted by courts. These instructions should be directed only at specific issues in the case and should not ramble. Juries should be permitted to take copies of the instructions with them into the jury room, or, if copies are not available, they should be permitted to tape record them and play them back any time a question of law arises. There is no reason why we should close our eyes to some of the great scientific advances of the twentieth century. The recording device is one that could well be used to improve jury instructions.

Conclusion. Jury instructions must be improved by using laymen's language and by making certain that they are addressed only to the specific issues of a case. It must be possible for the jury either to take a copy of the instructions or a taped record of them into the jury room, and to have full access to them at all times.

LIBERAL USE OF THE SPECIAL VERDICT

More than 350 years ago in the time of Lord Coke, this was stated as a legal maxim: "The most usual trial of matters of fact is by twelve such men and matters in law the judges ought to decide and discuss." This phrase in one form or another is still used over and over again: the facts are for the jury; the law is for the judge. In the normal general verdict this maxim is carried out rather simply. The judge tells the jury what the law is, the jury finds the facts and applies the law to them to arrive at a conclusion for plaintiff or defendant, which it then reports to the court. The general verdict has some limitations in cases involving complex problems. Learning the law is more complicated than merely listening to a judge's instruction and certainly the jury must learn the law if it is to apply it properly. Therefore, there may be wrong done when a jury fails to understand the law after instruction and erroneously applies it to the facts found.

In a great many of our states a procedure called the "special verdict" is used on occasion to permit the jury to do what it seems to be able to do best—find facts—and to permit the judge to find and apply the law. This procedure works very simply. The jury is given a small number of special questions about the ultimate facts which it answers. These questions and answers then become the basis for the final judgment of the court which applies the law to them. The matter of law application therefore is for the expert in the law rather than for the lay jury.

This device is sensible since it requires the jury to deliberate and find the facts, at the same time allowing them to apply community concepts and community ideas. This device will go a long way toward eliminating criticism which asserts that "twelve men can easily misunderstand more law in a minute than the judge can explain in an hour."

Conclusion. Serious consideration should be given to the use of the special verdict in all states.

BETTER TRAINING AND HIGHER STANDARDS FOR LAWYERS

Lawyers bear a great responsibility for the conduct of a trial. They frame the issues, produce the proof, examine the witnesses, and argue the case. In addition to this, they become the judges who conduct the trials. Besides their courtroom functions, they must be counselors and improvers of judicial administration, as well as leaders in their communities in other ways.

The trend in legal education today is to emphasize these latter functions of the lawyer rather than that of being an advocate. The law schools and the bar should pay more attention to the role of the lawyer in court, for the process of litigation suffers at times from inadequately prepared lawyers.

I suggest the following as a reasonable program for the education of lawyers as advocates. It is the program that is followed in substance at The University of Michigan Law School.

1. A sound groundwork should be given in procedural law. This should involve all aspects of the use of courts and other agencies for resolving disputes, the means by which cases get into courts, the methods by which they are carried forward, and by which they are tried.

2. Law students should be exposed to some study in the field of the psychology of truth-finding. Obviously one of the lawyer's aims in preparing for trial and in the trial itself is to ascertain the truth. The more he knows about this aspect of a problem, the more he will be able to help the jury.

3. Practice in advocacy should be given in a realistic practice court. By means of motion pictures it is easy to simulate situations from which litigation can arise. These pictures can be shown to prospective witnesses, each of which can be identified with a character in the film. The witnesses then can be made available to the student lawyers for interrogation and investigation, and the case can be investigated, pleaded, prepared, and tried in a realistic way.

4. It is essential that student lawyers be able to make critical analyses of common trials. There is no reason why courtrooms cannot be wired for closed circuit television so that their proceedings can be carried to law schools for observation and criticism. Such a program would produce lawyers capable of stepping into a courtroom and performing adequately, lawyers with the capability and desire to learn from other lawyers how to become truly accomplished advocates.

5. Legal education should not stop after law school. The last point I would suggest then is an expanded program of

continuing legal education in the field of trial practice. Lawyers must constantly keep alert to developments that will improve their techniques in bringing cases to a jury. Institutes and seminars should be available periodically so that lawyers can learn about new trial techniques.

Conclusion. Better advocates are needed to help the jury function more efficiently. More attention should be given to the preparation of advocates in law school and in programs of continuing legal education.

BETTER JUDGES

A judge is more than a moderator in a trial. He actually controls the whole litigious process. In a number of state and federal courts he not only has the power to instruct the jury on the law, but he also may advise them on the facts and set aside verdicts which he thinks are wrong. His every word and act in the courtroom is persuasive. Therefore, judges who have limited capacities for understanding the litigious process and a lack of appreciation for the adversary system can create difficulties for the jury in resolving disputes. Trials tend to drag on and errors are created which cause adverse reaction to the civil jury. Greater capability on the part of judges will make the jury function better. Evidence received will be more carefully controlled, analyses and statements of issues will be more accurate, and jury instructions will be clearer. In fact, the whole trial process will be carried on more effectively.

Although the selection of judges by popular election has produced for our judiciary some outstanding men, it also has sometimes produced men of mediocrity and of lesser quality. More attention must be paid to the process of selecting our judges. Since quality on the bench is not nearly so crucial in jury trials as it would be if all cases were decided by judges, this is less evident than it might otherwise be.

Conclusion. Very serious consideration should be given

to the adoption of methods of selecting judges that insure quality and provide for long tenure, so as to promote judicial independence of thought and action.

EVIDENCE RULES

The proof used by a jury to decide cases is presented during a trial according to rules of evidence that have become very technical indeed. These rules generally apply to both judge and jury trials alike. In a great many instances they hamper trials and create errors that are difficult to correct at the appeal stage. There is no need for this to happen today except for the fact that these rules have developed over a period of many years and inertia more than anything else has kept us from correcting them. If they could be corrected or brought up to date, not only jury trials but also all trials would be improved.

More than twenty years ago the American Law Institute suggested the adoption of a model code of evidence, and after a number of years of study it prepared such a code.[56] This code became the basis for further study by the Commissioners on Uniform State Laws who a number of years ago produced a set of 71 rules called the Uniform Rules of Evidence.[57] These rules are simplicity in themselves. They are based on the general theory that all relevant evidence is admissible with some exceptions, and they give a judge a great amount of discretion in the operation of a trial. If adopted, they would simplify the presentation of evidence to a very great extent, permitting juries to receive evidence that would be valuable to them. They are predicated to some extent upon the theory that our society as a whole is gradually becoming more sophisticated, more knowledgeable, and

[56] American Law Institute, MODEL CODE OF EVIDENCE, adopted at Philadelphia, 1942.

[57] UNIFORM RULES OF EVIDENCE, drafted by the National Conference of Commissioners on Uniform State Laws, approved Boston, 1953.

better educated, and that these qualities will be reflected in juries, thus making unnecessary technical, hamstringing rules to control trials. In this way trials would be facilitated and errors would be reduced.

Conclusion. All states should consider adoption of the Uniform Rules of Evidence.

DEMONSTRATIVE EVIDENCE

A lawyer is a teacher while he is in the courtroom, attempting to teach the judge and the jury what the facts of a case are in order that a verdict may be returned on behalf of his client. Effective teaching uses visual aids, such as blackboards, pictures, charts, graphs, maps, and so on. Lawyers use these visual aids, but sometimes they do not use them well enough or they use them aimlessly. Lawyers must give much more attention to the intelligent use of visual aids in presenting evidence, for these aids can be a great and necessary help to the jury in its difficult task.

Conclusion. Lawyers should be encouraged to present evidence by means of a more skillful use of visual aids since this will help the jury to understand better the issues and facts of a case.

ISSUES TRIED SEPARATELY

There are two underlying issues to every lawsuit. One deals with the liability of the defendant, the other with the amount of damages. In personal injury litigation very often these issues are separate from one another and ought to be considered separately by the fact-finders.

The ordinary method of trying lawsuits requires the plaintiff to produce all of his evidence on both issues, the defendant to produce all his evidence on both issues, and the jury to decide the case. Of course, if the decision is for the defendant, all of the evidence brought forward on the damage issue by the plaintiff has been a waste of time. It is also contended that often the evidence on the damage issue tends to color the decision on the liability issue. For example, a very bad injury may create sympathy and cause an unjustifiable finding for the plaintiff on the liability issue. The converse of this can also be true. Allegations of gross negligence or intentional wrongdoing often may accentuate modest injuries in the minds of the jury.

In Chicago's federal court a rule has been adopted permitting the trying of the liability and damage issues separately. The jury is first exposed to the evidence involving liability, upon which it bases a decision as to the liability. Only after this decision has been made is evidence brought forward pertaining to damages. The damage issue is then decided and the two verdicts are combined in a final judgment. This saves time in cases in which there are verdicts for the defendant since there is no need to present evidence on damage issues.

Conclusion. Consideration should be given to the adoption of a procedure permitting separate trials of issues of damage and liability in special cases.

VI

OPINIONS ABOUT THE CIVIL JURY

In 1830 Justice Story wrote: [58]

> *The trial by jury is justly dear to the American people. It has always been an object of deep interest and solicitude, and every encroachment upon it has been watched with great jealousy. . . . One of the strongest objections originally taken against the constitution of the United States, was the want of an express provision securing the right of trial by jury in civil cases. As soon as the constitution was adopted, this right was secured by the seventh amendment of the constitution proposed by congress; and which received an assent of the people so general, as to establish its importance as a fundamental guarantee of the rights and liberties of the people. . . .*

Do thoughtful lawyers and laymen still feel this way?

It seems fitting to conclude this paper with an examination of the opinions of others about the jury. The opinions of contemporary trial lawyers are reported in this chapter, while in the subsequent portion of the book the opinions of scholars, lawyers, and judges are recorded.

The popularity of the jury among laymen as a means of resolving disputes has already been reported by Mr. Kalven of the Chicago Jury Project. But what do lawyers who try cases think about juries? In preparing this paper I polled

[58] *Parsons v. Bedford, supra,* n. 39.

time." "It permits the only avenue to participation in government by people. It serves as a constant educational process and dignifies the judicial process." "In many cases where a party and particularly a plaintiff cannot recover as a matter of fact, we can best impress our citizens with the fairness of the final decision if we can point to the fact that a representative cross section of twelve neighbors decided that the party could not recover. We must do everything in our power to create confidence in our judges, courts, and the judicial system. The need is greater in the United States because of the lack of tradition which influences the actions of people such as the British." "It causes an awareness of a citizen's responsibility in governmental participation. I have had many jurors, particularly those with a small amount of education, say that serving as a juror was one of the outstanding events in their lives and that they would never forget it."

The lawyers were asked the following question: "Would you please give your opinion as to the fairness of jury verdicts compared with the decisions of trial judges in civil cases." Without exception, all of the lawyers responded that the decision of a jury is fairer than the decision of the trial judge. Typical comments included the following: "Jury verdicts tend to be more moderate, and the give and take by individual jurors in the jury room almost always results in a fair and just verdict. Of course, the individual backgrounds of the different jurors as contrasted with the background of a single trial judge, who is frequently aloof and out of touch with the community's feelings, reflect the thinking of the cross section of the community." "The varied experience and balanced moral code of twelve men is better than the experience of one cloistered judge." "It has been my experience that if a plaintiff in a personal injury case waives a jury trial the defendant will almost invariably demand a trial by jury. Apparently both parties in California would rather have their cases tried by a jury than by a judge because they believe that they will get a fairer trial. I believe this also." A jury is "generally more generous and kindly to persons seriously injured and handicapped in earning a living." "You sometimes hear defense counsel vehemently criticize the jury system because of a particular verdict by the jury. As a defense lawyer, I have been guilty of this offense on many occasions. When we view the jury verdict objectively, however, and particularly after a lapse of time when the heat of battle has subsided, we can honestly say that the jury did a pretty fair job. It is true that in some cases the jury deliberately disregards instructions and brings in a verdict that clearly reflects its passion and prejudice. On the other hand, I have tried many cases where the jury has brought in a verdict where a judge has later told me that I was extremely fortunate, because had he sat as a juror he would have brought in a verdict much larger than that of the jury. These statements have not been limited to state court judges who must stand for re-election. They have been made by federal court judges who presumably are unaffected by the emotional aspects of a trial."

Among active trial lawyers there seems to be a great amount of support for trial by jury in civil cases. The reasons given by these busy practitioners have been touched upon previously in this paper, and their testimony must be given substantial weight.

PART TWO

WHAT OTHERS SAY ABOUT THE JURY

VII

HOW THE JURY OPERATES IN OUR GOVERNMENT

CONTROL OF THE TRIAL JURY

The jury is a part of a government made up of the checks and balances of its three branches: the executive, legislative and judicial. The jury, as a part of the judicial branch of government, is devised to decide disputes and many safety factors are built into it to safeguard the integrity of the process. These are described by Professor Shartel together with a description of the checks and balances within the judicial system itself of which the jury is a part.

Checks and balances—separation and integration of powers
As I have already mentioned, a prominent feature of all the American constitutions, beginning with the federal, is the separation of governmental powers and acts into three kinds: legislative, executive, and judicial. This separation was not made by the framers of the Federal Constitution merely as a matter of convenient classification; it was made as a matter of policy. The founding fathers were deeply impressed by the argument of Montesquieu in his *Spirit of the*

Burke Shartel, Our Legal System and How It Operates. *From Michigan Legal Studies. Ann Arbor: University of Michigan Law School, 1951. Copyright 1951 by The University of Michigan. Reprinted with permission of the copyright owner. Foonotes have been omitted.*

Laws that such a separation is essential to the security and protection of the individual. Behind the separation of powers of government in this manner was a policy of checks and balances. The notion was that by creating three separate branches of government, each would serve as a check upon the acts and activities of the others. No one branch would be able to exceed or misuse its powers, inasmuch as it would be restrained by the powers and acts of the other two. In other words, the founders of our government expressed in the doctrine of separation of powers their intention to make the three branches of government independent for a special purpose—the purpose of using each branch as a means of insuring proper behavior, i.e., behavior according to standard, by the others.

Control of trial jury. The jury is part and parcel of our adjudicative machinery. Although its members are laymen and private citizens, the jury constitutes collectively an official agency. The function of the jury as it is ordinarily stated, is to find the facts. There are various standards which govern the jury's activities and procedures, such as the rule which forbids the jury to talk about the case to outside persons during the course of the trial, rules regarding burden of proof, etc. In the aggregate, the rules are all intended to insure a fair consideration and determination of the facts by the jury on the basis of the proofs which are presented to it. The effectuation of these standards for jury behavior presents many distinctive problems, which I believe it is desirable to discuss separately from problems regarding control of other official agencies involved in the adjudicative processes.

* * *

Theoretically, this combination of selective devices, starting with the preparation of a comprehensive jury list by an official agency, and followed by the drawing of a panel by lot, by exempting and excusing persons, and by striking off other persons for reasons of bias in the particular case, and finally by peremptory challenges, is supposed to result in a jury which is at one and the same time a cross section of the community, unbiased in its views, and satisfactory to all persons who are involved in the case to be tried. Actually, however, the average jury can hardly be said to represent a fair cross section of the community. Most of the ablest and busiest persons are able to avoid jury service by claiming exemptions or making excuses, and usually it is definitely to the interest of one party or the other to challenge the more intelligent jurors. The consequence is that only too often juries, especially in cities, are constituted of persons whose experience and capacity are below the average of the community. But I doubt if the remedy for this situation is to be found in the abandonment of jury trial—though as I have already pointed out, trial without jury is growing in popularity in some fields—rather the practical remedy for inferior juries is to be sought in better and more discriminating methods of selection, in reducing the number of exemptions and excuses, and in improving the pay and other conditions of jury service.

Inasmuch as the jury is made up of laymen, it cannot be expected to know the rules which are applicable to its official activities, the rules which apply to its weighing of evidence and its determination of facts. The judge always instructs the jury on request and, in fact, is required to instruct the jury as to its duties and procedures in determining the facts. But there are two kinds of verdicts which the jury may be required to give: a special verdict and a general verdict. A *special* verdict is a simple determination of facts which are disputed between the parties. Usually it takes the form of specific answers to specific questions of fact, e.g., "Did the defendant make such and such a promise?" and "Did the defendant perform this promise?" Such a verdict decides only fact questions and leaves to the judge the task of applying the law to the facts found. The functions of finding facts and of applying law are, in effect, completely separated. The *general* verdict is of quite a different sort; it represents the more common practice in this country. It is applicable to all criminal cases and is employed in most civil cases. In rendering a general verdict, the jury performs two functions; it determines the disputed facts and applies the law to them. For instance, in a case where D is charged with the theft of X's goods, and defends on the grounds that he took the goods believing they were his own, and that he was insane at the time of the act, the jury does not specifically report in its verdict whether D took the goods of X, and if so, whether he thought they were his own, or if he was insane at the time he took them; instead the jury declares simply that D was guilty or not guilty of the crime charged. Such a verdict obviously requires that the jury not only decide what happened, i.e., the facts, but also that it employ the rules of law applicable to what happened. This in turn makes it necessary that the jury be instructed about the rules of law applicable to the facts in issue. The court must tell the jury what the law requires it to do in connection with all the possible fact conclusions which it may justifiably reach on the evidence presented to it. This often calls for very elaborate instructions; and the jury is left with the task of applying them to the actual facts.

From what has already been said you will realize that the judge exercises a substantial control over the jury. Indeed, he controls the jury's performance of its functions in several important ways. First, he determines *what evidence* is to be admitted for the jury's consideration. He passes on the admissibility of this evidence, bit by bit, as it is presented. Second, he *instructs* the jury regarding its own functions and procedures, and regarding the law of the case where a general verdict is to be found. Third, the trial judge in the common law practice was accustomed to *comment* on the weight of the evidence; he gave the jury the benefit of his opinion and advice in relation to the facts of the case. This practice is still followed in the federal courts, and in a substantial number of state courts. However, in the majority of states this practice is no longer permitted; the judge is prohibited from indicating his opinion on the evidence in any way. Fourth, he is empowered to scrutinize the evidence which has been presented, and if he finds that the evidence on one side is altogether insufficient to support a verdict, he must *direct* the jury to find a *verdict* for the other side. As a recent writer says:

> *In present-day practice a directed verdict is a device for taking a case from the jury when there is no issue of fact for the jury to decide. The jury brings in a verdict, but it is clearly recognized that the act of the jury is merely a matter of form. This practice must be carefully distinguished from (1) instruction on the law and (2) advice on the facts.*

Fifth, the judge may *set aside* the jury's *verdict* if he concludes that it is contrary to the great weight of evidence, or is supported by insufficient evidence. Thus, if a jury has found D guilty of a crime, the judge may set this verdict aside if he finds that the verdict is based on insufficient evidence to justify a finding of guilt beyond a reasonable doubt.

In short, the judge supervises and checks the jury's fact-finding process in various ways just mentioned. The standards which require the jury to perform its functions in a certain manner are effectuated in a very real sense by this judicial control. However, it must not be supposed that the control of the judge over the jury's verdict is complete. The jury can ignore the judge's instructions with impunity. There was a time when juries in criminal cases were punishable for contempt in ignoring the court's instructions, and when juries in civil cases were liable to injured parties for returning improper verdicts. But for almost three centuries now it has been established in all Anglo-American jurisdictions that a jury cannot be penalized, criminally or civilly, for rendering a wrong or perverse verdict. And inasmuch as the jury has a wide range of discretion anyway, in drawing its conclusions of fact from the evidence, it must be apparent that the jury has considerable freedom of action. The standards which control the jury, like all other standards which we have discussed, are only partial in their coverage and are by no means completely enforceable. The judge's control merely represents elements of guidance and enforcement of standards within the limited range where enforcement is feasible. . . .

VIII

THE VALUE OF THE JURY

ON THE TRIAL BY JURY

Almost two centuries ago a famous English scholar extolled the virtue of jury trial as the savior of our liberty.

We may here, again, observe, and observing we can not but admire, how scrupulously delicate, and how impartially just the law of England approves itself, in the constitution and frame of a tribunal, thus excellently contrived for the test and investigation of truth; which appears most remarkably, 1. In the avoiding of frauds and secret management, by electing the twelve jurors out of the whole panel by lot. 2. In its caution against all partiality and bias, by quashing the whole panel or array, if the officer returning is suspected to be other than indifferent; and repelling particular jurors, if probable cause be shown of malice or favor to either party. The prodigious multitude of exceptions or challenges allowed to jurors, who are the judges of fact, amounts nearly to the same thing as was practiced in the Roman republic before she lost her liberty; that the select judges should be appointed by the prætor with the mutual consent of the parties. . . .

*　*　*

Sir William Blackstone, Commentaries on the Laws of England. *Vol. III. Adaptation by John L. Wendell. New York: Harper & Brothers, 1854. Footnotes have been omitted.*

Upon these accounts the trial by jury ever has been, and I trust ever will be, looked upon as the glory of English law. And if it has so great an advantage over others in regulating civil property, how much must that advantage be heightened when it is applied to criminal cases! But this we must refer to the ensuing book of these Commentaries; only observing, for the present, that it is the most transcendent privilege which any subject can enjoy or wish for, that he can not be affected either in his property, his liberty, or his person, but by the unanimous consent of twelve of his neighbors and equals. A constitution, I may venture to affirm has, under Providence, secured the just liberties of this nation for a long succession of ages. And, therefore, a celebrated French writer, who concludes that because Rome, Sparta, and Carthage have lost their liberties, therefore those of England in time must perish, should have recollected that Rome, Sparta, and Carthage, at the time when their liberties were lost, were strangers to the trial by jury.

Great as this eulogium may seem, it is no more than this admirable constitution, when traced to its principles, will be found in sober reason to deserve. The impartial administration of justice, which secures both our persons and our properties, is the great end of civil society. But if that be entirely intrusted to the magistracy, a select body of men, and those generally selected by the prince or such as enjoy the highest offices in the state, their decisions, in spite of their own natural integrity, will have frequently an involuntary bias toward those of their own rank and dignity: it is not to be expected from human nature that *the few* should be always attentive to the interests and good of *the many*. On the other hand, if the power of judicature were placed at random in the hands of the multitude, their decisions would be wild and capricious, and a new rule of action would be every day established in our courts. It is wisely, therefore, ordered that the principles and axioms of law, which are general propositions, flowing from abstracted reason, and not accommodated to times or to men, should be deposited in the breasts of the judges, to be occasionally applied to such facts as come properly ascertained before them. For here partiality can have little scope; the law is well known and is the same for all ranks and degrees: it follows as a regular conclusion from the premises of fact pre-established. But in settling and adjusting a question of fact, when intrusted to any single magistrate, partiality and injustice have an ample field to range in; either by boldly asserting that to be proved which is not so, or by more artfully suppressing some circumstances, stretching and warping others, and distinguishing away the remainder. Here, therefore, a competent number of sensible and upright jurymen, chosen by lot from among those of the middle rank, will be found the best investigators of truth, and the surest guardians of public justice. For the most powerful individual in the state will be cautious of committing any flagrant invasion of another's right, when he knows that the fact of his oppression must be examined and decided by twelve indifferent men, not appointed till the hour of trial; and that, when once the fact is ascertained, the law must of course redress it. This, therefore, preserves in the hands of the people that share which they ought to have in the administration of public justice, and prevents the encroachments of the more powerful and wealthy citizens. Every new tribunal, erected for the decision of facts, without the intervention of a jury (whether composed of justices of the peace, commissioners of the revenue, judges of a court of conscience, or any other standing magistrates), is a step toward establishing aristocracy, the most oppressive of absolute governments. The feodal system, which, for the sake of military subordination, pursued an aristocratical plan in all its arrangements of property, had been intolerable in times of peace, had it not been wisely counterpoised by that privilege, so universally diffused through every part of it, the trial by the feodal peers. And in every country on the Continent, as the trial by the peers has been gradually disused, so the nobles have increased in power, till the state has been torn to pieces by rival factions, and oligarchy, in effect, has been established, though under the shadow of regal government, unless where the miserable commons have taken shelter under absolute monarchy, as the lighter evil of the two. And, particularly, it is a circumstance well worthy an Englishman's observation, that in Sweden the trial by jury, that bulwark of northern liberty, which continued in its full vigor so lately as the middle of the last century, is now fallen into disuse; and that there, though the regal power is in no country so closely limited, yet the liberties of the commons are extinguished, and the government is degenerated into a mere aristocracy. It is, therefore, upon the whole, a duty which every man owes to his country, his friends, his posterity, and himself, to maintain to the utmost of his power this valuable constitution in all its rights; to restore it to its ancient dignity, if at all impaired by the different value of property, or otherwise deviated from its first institution; to amend it wherever it is defective; and, above all, to guard with the most jealous circumspection against the introduction of new and arbitrary methods of trial, which, under a variety of plausible pretenses, may in time imperceptibly undermine this best preservative of English liberty.

Yet, after all, it must be owned that the best and most effectual method to preserve and extend the trial by jury in practice would be by endeavoring to remove all the defects, as well as to improve the advantages, incident to this mode of inquiry. If justice is not done to the entire satisfaction of the people in this method of deciding facts, in spite of all encomiums and panegyrics on trials at the common law, they will resort in search of that justice to another tribunal; though more dilatory, though more expensive, though more arbitrary in its frame and constitution. If justice is not done to the crown by the verdict of a jury, the necessities of the public revenue will call for the erection of summary tribunals. . . .

TRIAL BY JURY IN THE UNITED STATES CONSIDERED AS A POLITICAL INSTITUTION

More than a century ago France's deTocqueville made his pointed and perceptive observations about American institutions. He was intrigued with the civil jury as a means of educating people, as a developer of the character of people, and as an education in government.

Since my subject has led me to speak of the administration of justice in the United States, I will not pass over it without adverting to the institution of the jury. Trial by jury may be considered in two separate points of view; as a judicial, and as a political institution. If it was my purpose to inquire how far trial by jury, especially in civil cases, insures a good administration of justice, I admit that its utility might be contested. As the jury was first established when society was in its infancy, and when courts of justice merely decided simple questions of fact, it is not an easy task to adapt it to the wants of a highly civilized community, when the mutual relations of men are multiplied to a surprising extent, and have assumed an enlightened and intellectual character.

My present purpose is to consider the jury as a political institution; any other course would divert me from my subject. Of trial by jury, considered as a judicial institution, I shall here say but little. When the English adopted trial by jury, they were a semi-barbarous people; they have since

Alexis de Tocqueville, Democracy in America. *Vol. I. Second Edition. (Translated by Henry Reeve; edited by Francis Bowen.) Cambridge: Sever and Francis, 1863. Footnotes have been omitted.*

become one of the most enlightened nations of the earth; and their attachment to this institution seems to have increased with their increasing cultivation. They have emigrated and colonized every part of the habitable globe; some have formed colonies, others independent states; the mother country has maintained its monarchical constitution; many of its offspring have founded powerful republics; but everywhere they have boasted of the privilege of trial by jury. They have established it, or hastened to re-establish it, in all their settlements. A judicial institution which thus obtains the suffrages of a great people for so long a series of ages, which is zealously reproduced at every stage of civilization, in all the climates of the earth, and under every form of human government, cannot be contrary to the spirit of justice.

But to leave this part of the subject. It would be a very narrow view to look upon the jury as a mere judicial institution; for, however great its influence may be upon the decisions of the courts, it is still greater on the destinies of society at large. The jury is, above all, a political institution, and it must be regarded in this light in order to be duly appreciated.

By the jury, I mean a certain number of citizens chosen by lot, and invested with a temporary right of judging. Trial by jury, as applied to the repression of crime, appears to me an eminently republican element in the government, for the following reasons.

The institution of the jury may be aristocratic or democratic, according to the class from which the jurors are taken; but it always preserves its republican character, in that it places the real direction of society in the hands of the governed, or of a portion of the governed, and not in that of the government. Force is never more than a transient element of success, and after force, comes the notion of right. A government which should be able to reach its enemies only upon a field of battle would soon be destroyed. The true sanction of political laws is to be found in penal legislation; and if that sanction be wanting, the law will sooner or later lose its cogency. He who punishes the criminal is therefore the real master of society. Now, the institution of the jury raises the people itself, or at least a class of citizens, to the bench of judges. The institution of the jury consequently invests the people, or that class of citizens, with the direction of society.

In England, the jury is returned from the aristocratic portion of the nation; the aristocracy makes the laws, applies the laws, and punishes infractions of the laws; everything is established upon a consistent footing, and England may with truth be said to constitute an aristocratic republic. In the United States, the same system is applied to the whole people. Every American citizen is qualified to be an elector, a juror, and is eligible to hold office. The system of the jury, as it is understood in America, appears to me to be as direct and as extreme a consequence of the sovereignty of the people as universal suffrage. They are two instruments of equal power, which contribute to the supremacy of the majority. All the sovereigns who have chosen to govern by their own authority, and to direct society instead of obeying its directions, have destroyed or enfeebled the institution of the jury. The Tudor monarchs sent to prison jurors who refused to convict, and Napoleon caused them to be selected by his agents.

* * *

I am so entirely convinced that the jury is pre-eminently a political institution, that I still consider it in this light when it is applied in civil causes. Laws are always unstable unless they are founded upon the manners of a nation:

manners are the only durable and resisting power in a people. When the jury is reserved for criminal offences, the people only witness its occasional action in particular cases: they come accustomed to do without it in the ordinary course of life; and it is considered as an instrument, but not as the only instrument, of obtaining justice. This is true *a fortiori,* when the jury is applied only to certain criminal causes.

When, on the contrary, the jury acts also on civil causes, its application is constantly visible; it affects all the interests of the community; every one co-operates in its work: it thus penetrates into all the usages of life, it fashions the human mind to its peculiar forms, and is gradually associated with the idea of justice itself.

The institution of the jury, if confined to criminal causes, is always in danger; but when once it is introduced into civil proceedings, it defies the aggressions of time and man. If it had been as easy to remove the jury from the manners as from the laws of England, it would have perished under the Tudors; and the civil jury did in reality, at that period, save the liberties of England. In whatever manner the jury be applied, it cannot fail to exercise a powerful influence upon the national character; but this influence is prodigiously increased when it is introduced into civil causes. The jury, and more especially the civil jury, serves to communicate the spirit of the judges to the minds of all the citizens; and this spirit, with the habits which attend it, is the soundest preparation for free institutions. It imbues all classes with a respect for the thing judged, and with the notion of right. If these two elements be removed, the love of independence becomes a mere destructive passion. It teaches men to practise equity; every man learns to judge his neighbor as he would himself be judged. And this is especially true of the jury in civil causes; for, whilst the number of persons who have reason to apprehend a criminal prosecution is small, every one is liable to have a lawsuit. The jury teaches every man not to recoil before the responsibility of his own actions, and impresses him with that manly confidence without which no political virtue can exist. It invests each citizen with a kind of magistracy; it makes them all feel the duties which they are bound to discharge towards society, and the part which they take in its government. By obliging men to turn their attention to other affairs than their own, it rubs off that private selfishness which is the rust of society.

The jury contributes powerfully to form the judgment and to increase the natural intelligence of a people; and this, in my opinion, is its greatest advantage. It may be regarded as a gratuitous public school, ever open, in which every juror learns his rights, enters into daily communication with the most learned and enlightened members of the upper classes, and becomes practically acquainted with the laws, which are brought within the reach of his capacity by the efforts of the bar, the advice of the judge, and even by the passions of the parties. I think that the practical intelligence and political good sense of the Americans are mainly attributable to the long use which they have made of the jury in civil causes.

I do not know whether the jury is useful to those who have lawsuits; but I am certain it is highly beneficial to those who judge them; and I look upon it as one of the most efficacious means for the education of the people which society can employ. . . .

THE VALUE OF THE JURY

In 1898 the president of the American Bar Association, distinguished trial lawyer Joseph H. Choate, devoted his annual address to the virtue of jury trial as an answer to criticisms of the system at that time.

Joseph H. Choate, "Annual Address." From Report of the Twenty-First Annual Meeting of the American Bar Association. *Vol. XXI. Philadelphia: Dando Printing and Publishing Company, 1898.*

The truth is, however, that the jury system is so fixed as an essential part of our political institutions; it has proved itself to be such an invaluable security for the enjoyment of life, liberty and property for so many centuries; it is so justly appreciated as the best and perhaps the only known means of admitting the people to a share, and maintaining their wholesome interest, in the administration of justice; it is such an indispensable factor in educating them in their personal and civil rights; it affords such a school and training in the law to the profession itself; and is so embedded in our constitutions which, as I have said, declare that it shall remain forever inviolate, requiring a convention or an amendment to alter it—that there can be no substantial ground for fear that any of us will live to see the people consent to give it up.

* * *

It is for the integrity, efficiency, and utility of trial by jury in civil causes that I am chiefly concerned, and would most earnestly plead today with my professional brethren, who are naturally responsible for public sentiment on such a subject. For I cherish, as the result of a life's work nearing its end, that the old-fashioned trial by a jury of twelve honest and intelligent citizens remains today, all suggested innovations and amendments to the contrary, the best and safest practical method for the determination of facts as the basis of judgment of courts, and that all attempts to tinker or tamper with it should be discouraged as disastrous to the public welfare.

You may say that I am contending for an ideal tribunal. On the contrary I speak for what is not only possible, but actually within the reach of every state and every community—ideal only for the purpose designed, as when we say that a particular man would make an ideal judge, an ideal senator, or an ideal general.

* * *

Well, the first and most essential element in a jury trial is a wise, learned, impartial, and competent judge—a judge qualified by his character, learning, and experience to preside over and control the proceedings, and to advise the jury as to the discharge of their duties. Add to the ordinary modicum of legal learning, courage, honesty, and common sense, and you have the kind of a judge I mean. If we say that an adequate supply of such judges possessed of these ordinary qualities of manhood cannot be found, we libel our own profession, we befoul our own nest wherein they are bred. Of course they cannot be had, if we apply to judicial nominations our favorite democratic idea that one man is as good as another for any office; of course they cannot be had if selected for partisan services; of course they cannot be had if appointed by a boss, or if they are required or allowed to pay for their nominations directly or indirectly; but they can be had if selected on their merits from the gladiators in this same arena, as England has selected her judges since 1688, always with assured success. They must be had, if our institutions are to be preserved.

And then there are the twelve honest and intelligent jurors drawn from the body of the community, sworn to pass upon the issue, and to return whence they came when their task is done. If we say that the average citizen is not equal to the duty, we belie our American manhood, we contradict the whole course of judicial history, and we fail of our duty to the communities of which we form a part, which rely upon us implicitly for the legislative machinery by which juries are to be secured.

And then you must have the earnest and loyal advocates, sworn to do their whole duty; which means to employ all their powers and attainments, and to use their utmost skill and eloquence, in exhibiting the merits each of his own side of the case. In doing so, as Mr. Justice Curtis well said, the advocate only does his duty, and if the adversary does his, the administration of justice is secured. I omit not the indispensable presence of the public, an ever essential feature in this great historic forum, for justice, though blind to the parties and to everything but the merits of the case, must never be secret. It is the sacred possession of the people in whose name and by whose authority it is done. Do you say again that this is an ideal picture? Who of you has not seen it? Who of you does not know that it is not only possible, but can be and ought to be the actual and every day scene in our Courts? I well remember witnessing such an administration of justice by Chief Justice Shaw and his associates in the Supreme Judicial Court of Massachusetts, aided uniformly by juries representing the best citizenship of that grand old State, and by a group of advocates whose superiors the world has never known, disposing of great causes in the presence of a bar instructed, and of a public educated, by the noble spectacle. I have witnessed the same scene in the city of New York under the administration of Chief Justice Oakley and Judge Duer and their associates, and coming down from those early days to the present I have seen it a hundred times since, down to the last term of our Federal Court when I saw an important and intricate cause disposed of by as good a jury as ever sat, under the guidance of a faithful and competent judge.

Are we willing to admit that the bench, the bar, the intelligence of the community from which the average juror is drawn, have so degenerated in the last fifty years, or in our generation, that this great tribunal, which has commanded the confidence and approval of all English speaking people for centuries, is no longer adequate for our public needs? For one I refuse to believe that. I know that the bar of today is adequate for the duties of today—that it can furnish material for the bench worthy of the great service of justice. And I feel quite sure that the average standard, not only of morals but of intelligence in our American communities which furnish our supply of jurors, has not receded but has actually advanced in the last half century.

This trial by jury for which I stand, is not only ancient as magistracy, rich in the traditions of freedom and of justice, glorified by the prestige and the prowess of all the great advocates of our race, but it is the proudest and most delightful privilege of our whole professional life. It alone atones for and mitigates all the drudgery and painful labor of the rest of our professional work. Here alone we feel the real joy of the contest, that *gaudium certaminis,* which is the true inspiration of advocacy. Here alone occur those sudden and unexpected conflicts of reason, of wit, of nerve, with our adversaries, with the judge, with the witnesses; those constant surprises, equal to the most startling in comedy or tragedy. Here alone is our one entertainment, in the confinement for life to hard labor, to which our choice of profession has sentenced us, and here alone do the people enter into our labors and lend their countenance to our struggles and triumphs. Sorry indeed for our profession will be the day when this best and brightest and most delightful function, which calls into play the highest qualities of heart, of intellect, of will, and of courage, shall cease to excite and to feed our ambition, our sympathy, and our loyalty.

* * *

The next formidable charge against the common law trial by jury is to accuse it of a great share in the law's delay. But I deny the charge absolutely and altogether. There is nothing in the whole realm of litigation so short, sharp, and decisive as the ordinary jury trial. From the first moment when the impanelling of the jury begins, down to the last when the verdict is recorded, there is no pause or interruption, except such as the natural wants of those concerned, for food and rest and sleep require. It would not be possible to devise a mode of trial which in its actual operation would more absolutely preclude delay. As compared with the abominable system of references which is the practical substitute for it, a trial by jury is like the lightning's flash. These references hang on for months and generally for years; they wear out the life blood of the parties, and pile up an accumulated mass of expense for the fees of lawyers, referees, and stenographers, fatal to the patience and endurance of clients. Why, I have one in my hands today which began in September, 1864, has survived both parties, all the witnesses, and a long succession of referees, and will still live on to be buried with the surviving counsel.

In these days too, when in trial by judge without a jury, written and printed briefs are to be submitted after the oral argument, indefinite delays ensue.

No, the charge of delay against juries and jury trials is wholly without foundation.

But there are most grievous delays, between the joining of issue of fact and the opportunity to try the case before a jury, and further grievous delays between a just and righteous verdict and the realization of the money or property represented by it—delays at both ends, for which the jury are in no wise responsible, and which are the direct result of vicious legal machinery, capable in a large degree of alleviation and cure. It is to these that I bespeak your most careful attention; for here, as it seems to me, this association owes a duty to the profession and to the community from the constant performance of which it ought not to shrink. . . .

* * *

The only other important defect attributed to the trial by jury as conducted from time immemorial, is the too prevalent notion that it permits to the trial judge too great a power in conducting the trial and guiding the deliberations of the jury. And so jealous have the people in some of the states become of such imputed interference of the judges with the functions of the jury, that in several states, instead of taking measures to improve their breed of judges, statutory contrivances have been devised to curtail and impair what seems to me to be the necessary function of the court, as an inherent part of the tribunal, without which its duties cannot be well and properly performed, whereby frequent failure of justice must eventually result. . . .

I can conceive of nothing better adapted than all such devices for mutilating and emasculating trial by jury, marring its symmetry, and destroying its utility as the best means of ascertaining the truth of the facts for judgment. That they are an unconstitutional invasion of the rights of the court and the people, in a state whose constitution like that of New York provides that trial by jury, in all cases in which it has been heretofore used, shall remain inviolate forever, may be claimed with great force and probable success. . . .

* * *

. . . But if your judges don't suit you, get better ones. Don't remove the ancient landmarks of the constitution and law, and turn trial by jury into a farce. There is no doubt that jurymen require such aid and assistance to enable them to perform their proper duty, and that whatever tends to deprive them of it, in whole or in part, to that extent weakens their capacity and impairs their usefulness.

* * *

But you will justly ask, is there no defect, no drawback, no decadence in this much boasted trial by jury? and is there no improvement, no remedy which you can suggest as the result of forty years experience, as a participant in this mode of trial? and you will very properly expect from me an answer to these questions.

Well, I do admit the existence in some degree of the very faults which I have been considering, but the result of my experience and observation has been, that in the general estimate their extent is grossly exaggerated, and if you have followed me thus far and read between the lines of my address, you have seen that I have no faith in the legislative remedies which have been experimentally applied, because they tend generally to impair the integrity, the efficiency, and the utility of this great and time honored tribunal, and because they do not propose—there has never yet been proposed—any adequate substitute to take its place.

But if you would have jury trial as it has been and ought still to be, if you would make it still worthy of the high encomiums which have been pronounced upon it by great jurists and great lawyers since 1688, and worthy of the confidence which it still enjoys with the great mass of the people, for whose security and safety all courts exist; if you would transmit it to posterity as a heritage from the past improved and not impaired by your keeping; there is an obvious and an open way. If you would have trial by jury as it has been exhibited in those wholesome and impressive instances to which I have referred, you must lend your aid to make the component parts of the tribunal what they can be, and should be, and to furnish better jurors, better judges, and better advocates to conduct the proceeding.

* * *

Give us then competent jurors, able judges, and honest, fearless, and learned advocates, and trial by Jury, which I am sure the people of America are determined to maintain, will still be the best safeguard of their lives, their liberties and their property.

* * *

THE LEGAL AND POLITICAL EFFECTS OF THE JURY SYSTEM

Sir William Holdsworth, the thoughtful English legal historian, emphasizes the value of the common practical touch which the jury brings to the fact-finding and decision-making process. He points out how sterile the adjudicative process would become without it.

The defects of the jury system are obvious. They are twelve ordinary men—"a group just large enough to destroy even the appearance of individual responsibility." They give no reasons for their verdict, which is perhaps apt, and it is apt, in times of political excitement, to reflect the popular prejudice of the day. Experience shows that they are capable of intimidation. It is said that they are always biased when a pretty woman or a railway company happen to be litigants. Though a good special jury is admitted to be a very competent tribunal, the common jury may be composed of persons who have neither the desire nor the capacity to weigh the evidence, or to arrive at a conclusion upon the facts in issue. But in spite of these obvious defects, distinguished judges, who have spent many years working with juries, have combined to praise the jury system. Fortescue, Coke, Hale, Blackstone, and Stephen are witnesses whose evidence should be conclusive. We may add to these names that of Chalmers,

Sir William Holdsworth, A History of English Law. *Vol. I, 7th ed. Revised under editorship of A. L. Goodhart and H. G. Hanbury. London: Methuen & Co. Ltd., 1956.* *Footnotes have been omitted.*

whose experience in the new county courts led him to the same conclusions. In fact the jury system works well from the point of view of the litigant, the judge, the jury itself, and the law.

The litigant gets a body of persons who bring average common sense to bear upon the facts of his case. "A jury," says Chalmers, "is a far better tribunal than a judge for dealing with questions of fact. The more I see of juries the higher is the respect I have for their decisions. . . . They have a marvellous faculty for scenting out a fraud." Their findings create no precedent; and thus they can decide hard cases equitably without making bad law. Litigants are generally contented with the measure of justice which they mete out; and this is no small gain to a legal system.

Judges have, as we have seen, from the earliest times appreciated the relief from responsibility which the jury system affords to them. Both Hale and Stephen emphasize this fact. And not only does the collaboration of the jury relieve the judge from the responsibility of deciding simply upon his own opinion, it also helps him to take, as the adviser and director of the jury, a more truly judicial attitude. Thus it helps to preserve the dignity of the Bench; for, if the judge preserves this judicial attitude, no odium can attach to him whatever be the verdict of the jury. And so, as de Tocqueville has said, "the jury which seems to diminish the power of the magistrate really gives it its pre-eminent authority."

The jury itself is educated by the part which it is required to take in the administration of justice. The jury system teaches the members of the jury to cultivate a judicial habit of mind. It helps to create in them a respect for law and order. It makes them feel that they owe duties to society, and that they have a share in its government. It is this education of the members of the jury that de Tocqueville regarded as the most valuable consequence of the system. "We should regard it as a school which gives instruction gratuitously and continuously. Where each juryman can learn his rights, where he mixes day by day with the best educated and most enlightened of the upper classes, where the law is taught to him in the most practical way, and is explained in a manner which he can understand by the efforts of the bar, by the direction of the judge, and even by the passions of the parties."

The effects of the jury system upon the law are no less remarkable and no less beneficial. It tends to make the law intelligible by keeping it in touch with the common facts of life. The reasons why and the manner in which it thus affects the law are somewhat as follows: If a clever man is left to decide by himself disputed questions of fact he is usually not content simply to decide each case as it arises. He constructs theories for the decision of analogous cases. These theories are discussed, doubted, or developed by other clever men when such cases come before them. The interest is apt to centre, not in the dry task of deciding the case before the court, but rather in the construction of new theories, the reconciliation of conflicting cases, the demolition or criticism of older views. The result is a series of carefully constructed, and periodically considered rules, which merely retard the attainment of a conclusion without assisting in its formation. It is only the philosopher, or possibly the professor of general jurisprudence, who can pursue indefinitely these interesting processes. Rules of law must struggle for existence in the strong air of practical life. Rules which are so refined that they bear but a small relation to the world of sense will sooner or later be swept away. Sooner, if like the criminal law or the commercial law, they touch nearly men's habits and conduct; later, if like the law of real property, they affect a smaller class, and affect them less nearly. The jury system has for some hundreds of years been constantly bringing the rules of law to the touchstone of contemporary common sense. The beneficial effects of this process can be best illustrated by a comparison with some of the rules evolved by the court of Chancery which never worked with a jury. "One finds oneself," says Chalmers, "in a rarified atmosphere of morality and respectability in which life is hardly possible. Look at the equitable doctrines of constructive notice and constructive fraud. Look at the impossible standard of duty laid down for trustees." The legislature has done something to remedy these things. Most perhaps was done by Sir George Jessel who was a profound equity lawyer with the mind of an acute juryman. He did much to bring the rules of equity to the touchstone of common sense; and his influence has been felt by all his successors.

Judges must explain the law to the jury. They must separate the rule of law from the question of fact. This produces both precision in the statement of the rule, and a clear outside judgment on the facts. Bagehot said of the Parliamentary head of a government office, "his function is to bring a representative of outside sense and outside animation in contact with the inside world. No man is a perfect representative of outside sense . . . that many-sided sense finds no microcosm in any single individual." The jury is to the inside technical world of our common law system a representative of that outside sense, and outside animation.

TRIAL BY JURY

A distinguished English barrister and judge, Sir Patrick Devlin, speaking recently, has emphasized the fact that the jury verdict more closely approximates a meritorious decision than does the decision of a judge; that the jury tempers with equity, the harshness of legal doctrine, safeguards the independence of the judge, protects the public against repugnant laws, and acts as the ultimate protector of our individual liberties.

Sir Patrick Devlin. "Trial by Jury." The Hamlyn Lectures, *8th series. London: Stevens & Sons Limited, 1956. Copyright 1956. Reprinted with permission of the copyright owner. Footnotes have been omitted.*

. . . Is the mode of trial, by judge and jury combined, better than trial by judge alone? I do not think that that question can be answered without asking a counter-question: tell me what sort of justice you want to get and I shall tell you which mode of trial is more likely to get it. Is there then more than one sort of justice? Yes: the justice of the case is the best compromise that can be obtained between the demands of the law and judgment on the merits. Those two points are always separated by some distance, long or short, and justice can be brought to rest anywhere between them; almost inevitably it will be nearer the one than the other. "But," a judge may say, "this is really not so. I try many cases in which no legal technicalities are involved and in which I deliver a judgment on the merits that I am quite satisfied complies with the law. Take the common accident case in which an employer is said to have been careless about a workman's safety; I have only to decide, entirely on the merits, whether carelessness on the part of the management or of the workman—or, if both, in what proportions—contributed to the accident." It is quite true that that is a judgment on the merits, but it is not a judgment on all the merits, only on those that the law permits the judge to consider. The only question of liability that the law allows to be discussed is whether one or both were careless. It is irrelevant that the employer is in a small business and that he personally took all the care he could, the fault being that of some workman for whom he was responsible. If the management was not careless, it is irrelevant that the workman was injured because he took a risk in an attempt to shorten the job and so save his employer money; he may have given long and faithful service to his employer and the injury may have crippled him for life, but that will avail him nothing. An ordinary man, not bound by the law and taking all the circumstances into consideration, might in such a case easily end up by saying: "Well, his employer can well afford to pay him something."

Observe that I am not contrasting law and justice. I am

contrasting a judgment according to law with a judgment according to the merits. Judgments according to the merits do not necessarily make justice. They would do so if there were only one judge and he always remembered to decide everything the same way and he went on living forever—in short, if justice on earth were divine and not human. But for human justice the law is indispensable. If, on substantially the same set of facts, one workman succeeded and another did not, it would rightly be said to be unjust that the one should be given compensation and the other not. It is an essential attribute of justice in a community that similar decisions should be given in similar cases. But that can be done only by following the law. It would not do if one judge were to deem it just that workmen should be compensated by their employer for all injuries incurred in his service, while another deemed it just that an employer should be responsible only for his own personal carelessness. So the law gives the general rule. No general rule ever fits exactly any particular case. A just decision is as much an abstract notion as the average duration of life. The average life of an Englishman is known to a fraction of a second, but anyone who expired at the correct moment would deserve to be entombed beneath a mortality table. If I were commissioning a statue to represent justice, I should not stipulate for a lady with ample draperies and a pair of scales: I should ask a sculptor of the modern school to design an embodiment of Colonel Bogey.

This is why ministers of justice have to serve two mistresses—the law and the *aequum et bonum* or the equity of the case. Their constant endeavour is to please both. That is why the just decision fluctuates, as I say, between two points. In most systems the just decision is tied pretty closely to the law; the law may be made as flexible as possible, but the justice of the case cannot go beyond the furthest point to which the law can be stretched. Trial by jury is a unique institution, devised deliberately or accidentally—that is, its origin is accidental and its retention deliberate—to enable justice to go beyond that point. The essentials of the device are that the tribunal consists of a comparatively large body of men who have to do justice in only a few cases once or twice in their lives, to whom the law means something but not everything, who are anonymous and who give their decision in a word and without a reason.

The fact that juries pay regard to considerations which the law requires them to ignore is generally accepted. I do not mean by that that they frequently and openly flout the law, but that they do not always succeed in separating the wheat from the chaff. Certainly a jury is not as good a separating machine as a judge would be; and the reason why a jury is to be preferred in some cases is because there are some cases in which a little admixture of chaff is not a bad thing. It is, for example, generally accepted that a jury will tend to favour a poor man against a rich man: that must be because at the bottom of the communal sense of justice there is a feeling that a rich man can afford to be less indifferent to the misfortunes of others than a poor man can be. There is no doubt, likewise, that juries, however often they may be told that they are not to have regard to the consequences of their verdict, do take the penalty into consideration, and have always done so, particularly if it is the death penalty. An interesting recognition of the jury's aptitude for going beyond the law is to be found in the evidence given to the Royal Commission on Capital Punishment 1949–1953 by those who favoured the retention of the M'Naghten Rules on insanity while agreeing that in some cases their application might be too rigid. Lord Chief Justice Goddard said: "I think a jury can always be trusted to do justice where it might be impossible to bring the case strictly within the M'Naghten Rules." Lord Simon, a former Lord Chancellor, said that in practice the Rules were qualified and added: "A British jury, whatever you say, will see that it is qualified if they are really convinced that it is a proper case."

Predictability v. Uncertainty

The essential virtue then of trial by jury is that it is a mode of trial whereby the law, while remaining generally in control of the decision, loosens its grip on it so as to allow it to move nearer than it could otherwise do towards the *aequum et bonum*. Of course the jury cannot be allowed to stray too far from legal principles. Theoretically it is not recognised that they should stray at all: the system works by a practical acceptance of the fact that jurors will be jurors. There are disadvantages attached to this. You cannot move away from the law without sacrificing some of the virtues inherent in law; the further you move away from the law the less predictable the decision becomes. If justice were divine, predictability would be irrelevant: the divine law is clear and simple and an all-seeing judge would in the twinkle of an eye divide the sheep from the goats. But human justice is not concerned simply with good and evil. Justice in civil matters is often simply a process of adjustment which has not got to bestow serious blame on anyone but to determine how the consequences of an unfortunate act ought to be paid for. The process of adjustment cannot be performed in the twinkling of an eye but is inevitably an expensive one. A man will legitimately want to know in advance what the judgment is likely to be so that he may decide whether to incur costs in disputing a claim or to offer a sum in settlement. At an earlier stage he may want to know whether, if he does an act, he is likely to be held liable at all. One of the services which the law does for a community is to enable such questions to be answered with some accuracy; the further the process moves from the strict application of the law the more uncertain the advice will be. If you want certainty or predictability, you must keep the judgment running close to the law. If you want the best judgment in the light of all the facts when they have emerged, then it will be one that has moved nearer to the *aequum et bonum*. The unique merit of the jury system is, that it allows a decision near to the *aequum et bonum* to be given without injuring the fabric of the law, for the verdict of a jury can make no impact on the law.

But such a decision may well injure the element of predictability, which has rightly a part to play in the administration of justice; and so you will find that in modern times the mode of trial is allowed to depend upon the importance of that element in relation to the type of case that is being tried. When, for example, a man is on trial for his liberty, predictability is quite unimportant. What is then wanted is a decision on the merits that will after the event satisfy the public that justice as the ordinary man understands it has been done. Likewise, when a man's honour or reputation is at stake, he is more concerned to have a judgment that fits his merits than to weigh the probable cost of a lawsuit against the offer of a compromise. In any case in which there is going to be hard swearing on both sides, the result is unpredictable anyway until the witnesses have been heard and compared. Cases which have one or more of these characteristics will be probably either criminal or, if civil, will fall into one of the categories in which trial by jury is given as of right. If the case is of a common type in which there is no hot dispute on the facts—for example, the ordinary accident case on the roads or in the factories; there is often an acute conflict on certain parts of the evidence but rarely wholesale perjury—a jury is not normally allowed, unless the case has some exceptional feature: otherwise, if a jury were allowed in one, it would have to be allowed in all. The exceptional feature is very often that the injuries are unusually severe. Thus I think it will be found that the cases in which trial by jury is ordered—whether the order is made under a claim of right or in accordance with the general principles by which the discretion is exercised—are those in which for one reason or another it is specially important to one or other of the parties that he should have a judgment that fits the merits of his particular case. In discriminating in this manner, the law and the practice are, consciously or unconsciously, following the traditional way that I have already traced. The judges have always tried to reserve general matters for themselves and to leave to juries those which turn on the circumstances of the particular case. It is in this sphere that trial by jury excels. It is true that the figures I have given you show that in civil cases it is comparatively little used. That does not suggest to my mind that it is an inferior instrument but rather that the civil cases to which it is best adapted are at the present time, as it happens, comparatively rare.

Jury as Safeguard of Independence and Quality of Judges

This is all that I have to say about the jury as an instrument for doing justice. But its value does not lie solely in the fact that for some cases it is the best judicial instrument. It serves two other purposes of great importance in the constitution. The first and lesser of these is that the existence of trial by jury helps to ensure the independence and quality of the judges. Judges are appointed by the executive and I do not know of any better way of appointing them. But our history has shown that the executive has found it much easier to find judges who will do what it wants than it has to find amenable juries. Blackstone, whose time was not so far removed from that of the Stuarts, thought of the jury as a safeguard against "the violence and partiality of judges appointed by the Crown." Commenting on that in 1784, Mr. Justice Willes said: "I am sure no danger of this sort is to be apprehended from the judges of the present age: but in our determinations it will be prudent to look forward into futurity." Although in 1956 we may claim that "futurity" has not yet arrived, it still remains prudent to look forward into it.

I spoke of the quality of the judges as well as of their independence. I did not mean by that their quality as lawyers or even as virtuous men: that must be left to the Lord Chancellor. I meant their quality as purveyors of the sort of justice that the Englishman wants to have. The malady that sooner or later affects most men of a profession is that they tend to construct a mystique that cuts them off from the common man. Judges, as much as any other professional, need constantly to remind themselves of that. For more than seven out of the eight centuries during which the judges of the common law have administered justice in this country, trial by jury ensured that Englishmen got the sort of justice they liked and not the sort of justice that the government or the lawyers or any body of experts thought was good for them. The very high percentage of non-jury cases in the civil lists, coupled with the fact that there is no great pressure for trial by jury, entitles the judges to claim that the justice they dispense is still, in the best sense of the word, popular justice. But it is well to remember that if judges ceased to be popular, if their outlook became remote from that of the ordinary man, trial by jury is there as the alternative.

Jury as Safeguard against Repugnant Laws

The second and by far the greater purpose that is served by trial by jury is that it gives protection against laws which the ordinary man may regard as harsh and oppressive. I do not mean by that no more than that it is a protection against tyranny. It is that: but it is also an insurance that the criminal law will conform to the ordinary man's idea of what is fair and just. If it does not, the jury will not be a party to its enforcement. They have in the past used their power of acquittal to defeat the full operation of laws which they thought to be too hard. I daresay that the cases in which a jury defies the law are very rare. Juries do not deliberately marshal legal considerations on one side and broader considerations of justice and mercy on the other and bring them into conflict on the field of conscience. Their minds are not trained to the making of an orderly separation and opposition; they are more likely to allow one set of considerations to act upon the other in such a way as to confuse the issues. One way or another they are prone to give effect to their repugnance to a law by refusing to convict under it, and no one can say them nay. The small body of men, who under modern conditions constitute the effective body of legislators, have to bear this in mind. It affects the character of the laws they make, for it is no use making laws which will not be enforced. They may put it down to the perversity of juries, though for my part I think that if there is a law which the juryman constantly shows by his verdicts that he dislikes, it is worth examining the law to see if there is something wrong with it rather than with the juryman. I do not mean that juries are altogether blameless in this respect; I have already recorded the opinions of two eminent judges on juries and the traffic laws. Juries are not often too tender to the wicked but they sometimes are to the foolish. I think that a juryman, if he can visualise the possibility of finding himself in the same situation as the man in the dock, finds it very difficult to be firm; it is an inevitable defect of the system that jurymen are not practised in detachment. It may be, therefore, that the jury system means that some good and necessary laws are only weakly enforced. Likewise, democracy may mean that some good and necessary measures of government are not taken when they should be. There are no freedoms to be got without payment.

* * *

Jury as Lamp of Freedom

Each jury is a little parliament. The jury sense is the parliamentary sense. I cannot see the one dying and the other surviving. The first object of any tyrant in Whitehall would be to make Parliament utterly subservient to his will; and the next to overthrow or diminish trial by jury, for no tyrant could afford to leave a subject's freedom in the hands of twelve of his countrymen. So that trial by jury is more than an instrument of justice and more than one wheel of the constitution: it is the lamp that shows that freedom lives. To many of us the boundaries between Whitehall and Westminster are uncertain and confused. We are anxious that government should be strong and yet fearful lest the gathering momentum of executive power crush all else that is in our State. We look for some landmark that we may say that so long as it stands, we are safe; and if it is threatened, we must resist. It is there, this beacon that seven centuries have tended:

> *Nullus liber homo capiatur, vel imprisonetur, aut dissaisiatur, aut utlagetur, aut exuletur, aut aliquo modo destruatur, nec super eum ibimus, nec super eum mittemus, nisi per legale judicium parium suorum vel per legem terrae.*

These are the words of the Great Charter which Blackstone said secured to every Englishman that trial by his peers which is the grand bulwark of his liberties; and which he took as the text for one of the most celebrated passages in the *Commentaries*. His words today are still after two centuries as fresh and meaningful as when they were written and I wish in closing this subject to commend them to you.

> *So that the liberties of England cannot but subsist so long as this palladium remains sacred and inviolate; not only from all open attacks (which none will be so hardy as to make), but also from all secret machinations, which may sap and undermine it; by introducing new and arbitrary methods of trial; by justices of the peace, commissioners of the revenue, and courts of conscience. And however convenient these may appear at first (as doubtless all arbitrary powers, well executed, are the most convenient), yet let it be again remembered, that delays and little inconveniences in the forms*

of justice, are the price that all free nations must pay for their liberty in more substantial matters; that these inroads upon this sacred bulwark of the nation are fundamentally opposite to the spirit of our constitution; and that, though begun in trifles, the precedent may gradually increase and spread, to the utter disuse of juries in questions of the most momentous concern.

FUNCTION OF THE CIVIL JURY

An experienced American trial lawyer and judge asserts that the rules of trial, growing up because of the jury, are responsible for unmasking the liar and the thoughtless untruth teller. He also argues that the common judgment of twelve is more likely to be good and accurate than that of a single judge.

Function of the Civil Jury

Litigation, and indeed the legal profession, would be of no consequence in the lives of men if there existed some mechanical or scientific method of determining objectively what in fact had occurred upon the occasion giving rise to a dispute between human beings. Even in the fields of pure science, the investigator's conclusions are not infallible, and the law is anything but a laboratory of pure science. By and large, in order to discover what has happened in a situation involving human beings, we must rely upon what human beings say. I needn't belabor, to a group of trial lawyers, the problem of the difference between the testimony of honest witnesses describing the same event. Honest variations in testimony arise from the differences in witnesses' sense perceptions, their memories, their abilities to articulate, and a host of other factors. In fact, so fundamental are these differences that identical testimony by two witnesses is frequently

David N. Edelstein, "A Kind Word for the Civil Jury," 17 NACCA L. J. 302 (May, 1956). Reprinted with permission of the copyright owner.

suspect. At the very best, the law is at the mercy of the lowest common denominator of human frailties in any attempt to get at the truth. And at the worst the law is at the mercy of falsehood, in its almost infinitely varying degrees. It is difficult enough to piece together a story on the basis of honest testimony, but it is indescribably more difficult to bear in addition the burden of determining credibility. The [legal] writer [Sergeant] Stephen observed that "The natural and acquired shrewdness and experience by which an observant man forms an opinion as to whether a witness is or is not lying, is by far the most important of all a judge's qualifications, infinitely more important than any acquaintance with law or with rules of evidence. . . . This preeminently important power for a judge," he continued, "is not to be learnt out of books. Insofar as it can be acquired at all, it is to be acquired only by experience, for the acquisition of which the position of a judge is by no means peculiarly favorable. . . . Every one must learn matters of this sort himself, and though no sort of knowledge is so important to a judge, no rules can be laid down for its acquisition. . . . No process is gone through, the correctness of which can be independently tested. The judge has nothing to trust but his own natural and acquired sagacity."

My own experience has been a verification of these wise words. The determination of what to believe is a problem that runs the whole gamut between witnesses who are honestly motivated and those who are deliberately lying, and it is one of infinite difficulty. Although that determination is by far the most difficult problem in the law, it is not a legal problem. A view of witnesses from the bench affords no advantage over a view from the jury box. The view presented is a view of people, and the problem presented is one of judging people. This judgment, as Kent put it, "does not require a master's skill in the science of the law. It depends more on a knowledge of the passions and of the springs of human action and may be the lot of ordinary experience and sagacity."

But the determination of what to believe as a matter of fact must be followed by the making of a decision. As difficult as the process of fact-finding is, the decision does not follow mechanically or automatically. Thayer and Holmes engaged in a memorable dispute about the nature of the jury function in a negligence case. The issue was what is involved in a jury's application of the reasonable man standard to the facts as found. Thayer felt that this involved merely a further inference of fact, but Holmes held that each case involved a determination of the standard of conduct, and was thereby a temporary surrender of the judicial function. It is hardly to be doubted that this process is not one chained exclusively to the evidence. The juror selects from among his experiences those which he chooses to regard as normative. In applying the facts he has found to a rule of law he may, and indeed must, refer to a whole complex of additional concepts and attitudes, personal and impersonal, conscious and unconscious, articulate and inarticulate.

Superiority of Jury over Judge in Both Fact-Determination and Fixing the Standard of Conduct

Thus we have the two main elements of the jury's job: the determination of what facts to believe and the making of a decision based on those facts. For neither job is there a determining rule, and for neither job is a judge peculiarly qualified by reason of his position and experience. And it is my opinion that twelve jurors can do these jobs better, in the long run, than one judge.

As G. K. Chesterton was quoted by Judge Peck recently, "I would trust twelve ordinary men, but I cannot trust one ordinary man." I suppose there is no spiritual significance to the number twelve, although Lords Coke and Summers tell us that the number was chosen: "Like the prophets were twelve to foretell the truth; the apostles twelve to preach the truth; the discovers twelve, sent into Canaan to seek and report the truth; and the stones twelve that the Heavenly Hierusalem is built on." I would not go so far as to claim holy sanction for the number, but I do claim the sanction of reason and experience for a number substantially greater than one. Are not all appellate tribunals composed of several judges? And if we need a variety of minds to give us, in the long run, the most dependable judgments on supposedly definite rules of law, how much more do we need a variety of minds to give us dependable judgments on indefinite masses of facts? It cannot be denied that judicial opinions, from the lowest to the highest courts, represent in some measure the personal impulses of the judge, in relation to the situation before him, and that these impulses are determined by the judge's lifelong series of previous experiences, reflecting his temperament, personality, education, and environment. If that applies at all to the legal opinions of a judge, how much more it must apply to the decisions of a judge functioning as a jury. I do not mean to imply that judges are peculiarly subject to the influences of their backgrounds and value standards. But backgrounds and value standards are not altered when one puts on a judicial robe. Furthermore, a judge's personal values may be perpetuated and codified into a system. The ritualistic practices of our profession, leaning so heavily upon precedent and codification, render that a particularly likely danger. The occupational hazard of the judiciary is hardening of the categories, and when a judge sees similar situations before him, time and time again, year after year, they may, unconsciously on his part, merge into one. Certainly, all of you are familiar with the biases of some individual trial judges, and for all I know, with some of mine.

Obviously, I do not mean to imply that jurors are less subject to influence by personal idiosyncrasies and value standards. But that is precisely the point. With twelve of them, it seems to me, there is less likelihood that a verdict may be distorted by the personality factor of any one juror, and that there is more likelihood of a qualitatively better verdict based on the reconciliation of twelve varied temperaments and minds. Moreover, a jury of twelve brings a valuable array of experience in the problems of mankind and of acquaintance with the trials and obstacles that confront men in the pursuit of life, peace, and security. No single judge, I venture to say, can bring to bear so varied and valuable an experience as can any jury. Wigmore suggested the experiment of inviting twelve intelligent friends, some evening, to your house, and asking them any question of opinion or fact, calling for serious thought—a question of politics, business, morals, health, science, recreation, or what you like. "Will it ever happen," he asked, "that you do not glean from at least two or three of the twelve some argument or detail or judgment that the others (if they were agreed) had failed to mention?" And is not this precisely the virtue that is of supreme significance in the discharge of the two cardinal responsibilities of determining, in a trial, what facts are worthy of belief and the making of a decision based on those facts? The great Holmes did not think so. He wrote, in "The Common Law," "A Judge who has long sat at *nisi prius* ought gradually to acquire a fund of experience which enables him to represent the common sense of the community in the ordinary instances far better than the average jury. Furthermore, the sphere in which he is able to rule, without taking their opinion at all, should be continually growing." With the utmost of deference to that giant of our jurisprudence, that has not been my experience. Of course, I have not long sat on the trial bench, and perhaps when I shall have, I shall change my mind. But my present experience teaches me a greater respect for the jury's capacity than for my own in the performance of the functions I have described.

Indictment of the Civil Jury

All of this, the antagonist of the civil jury may reply, is very interesting theoretical twaddle. For the jury's verdict has very little to do with the facts or the law or the judge or any of the virtues of mankind. It is said that the jury is a law unto itself, deciding by whim, chance, or chicanery. A verdict may be returned by a juror who has slept through the testimony, as the result of the flip of a coin, or in order to get home quickly. Jurors consider matters prohibited by their oaths and they permit their verdicts to be rendered in obedience to their prejudices or sympathies, regardless of their duty; they discard the legal rules and the evidence and bring in a verdict out of their own heads or hearts. Even if they should try to follow the judge's instructions, they probably couldn't because they consist mostly, in Judge Jerome Frank's words, of "ineffective rigmaroles, incantations, or semi-magical rituals which the judge utters to the jury's uncomprehending ears."

That is quite an indictment of the civil jury, and it is delivered in deadly earnest by highly respectable authorities in no inconsiderable numbers. Of course, it's a pretty difficult indictment to prove. I get the impression that the proof is presented in the vein of *res ipsa loquitur,* but it reaches me only in the vein of *ipse dixit.* My own experience with my juries has been satisfactory. I don't know what goes on in the jury room, and I shudder to think of the obvious suggestion to remedy that void. But until such a time comes, if it ever does, when we can know precisely how a jury behaves, I am convinced from my own experience with juries that they behave themselves very well indeed.

Appraisal of Criticism of the Jury System

As a judge who takes great pains with his jury charges, I must concede reluctantly that they are not frequently models of clarity and conciseness. On the other hand, I fervently hope that they cannot, by and large, be characterized in the playwright Channing Pollock's words as "grand conglomerations of garbled verbiage and verbal garbage." In any event, I can report that juries listen intently. They seem to understand. By their questions, sent out from the jury room, they often indicate that they understand. And by their requests for repetitions of less admirably phrased portions, they also indicate what they don't understand and request clarification. Along with Judge Goodman of the United States District Court for the Northern District of California, I venture to be skeptical about whether there is any basis in fact for the flat statement, so often and positively repeated, that juries frequently pay no heed to what the judge tells them to do. And along with Judge Goodman, I am also quite curious about the kind of evidence the other charges are based upon: namely that verdicts are often arrived at by the flip of a coin or because the jurors want to get home. I wonder whether these statements are based upon actual investigation or whether they are made for dramatic value. Not ever having had a tap on any of my juries, I can't make any categorical denials, but I personally have never heard a reliable report of such an incident. In fact, to cite a personal experience, which proves absolutely nothing, I was once the intermediary between a woman juror and her harassed husband on the subject of what to do with the chicken in the oven so as to get it ready for his and the children's supper. I spoke to her afterwards and she hadn't the slightest intention of shortchanging her jury responsibilities for the benefit of her domestic responsibilities.

Of course jurors, like other human beings, make mistakes. But their mistakes are in no different a category from the mistakes that may be made by legislators, administrators, and judges which equally may affect the life and security of the individual citizen. I can only insist that I am well satisfied that the juries in my experience have acted responsibly, in accordance with the oaths they have taken.

Capacity of Jury to Handle Complex Issues

But ascribing to the jury the most honorable of motivation and intention, it may be said that in cases which relate to such matters as commerce, mechanics, science, and medicine, the isues are invariably beyond the comprehension of the average juror. How can a mere voter be expected to decide intelligently whether a steamship has been equipped with proper machinery? How can a mechanic, however well-intentioned, judge the propriety of an unsuccessful surgical operation? Is a housewife capable of weighing the testimony of rival geologists? Those are fair questions, but I should like to put one more fair question. How can a mere judge, however well-intentioned, resolve all of these problems? If our trials present technical and scientific questions for resolution, I submit that a judge is not in enough of a better position to resolve them to make any substantial difference, if he is in a better position at all. It seems to me that the issue is not one between judge and jury, but between adversary and neutral presentation of expert testimony. I am not convinced that the usual battle of the experts presents an undue challenge to the jury. If it does, it presents a quite similar challenge to the judge. And if this is thought to be a serious problem, then there appears to be no sufficiently strong reason against providing that experts in the various specialized fields should be chosen not by the parties litigant but by the court, and not at random, but from a carefully compiled panel of properly qualified authorities approved beforehand by the respective scientific associations involved. I am not entirely convinced that this would be a wise solution to the problem. Nevertheless, as between judge and jury the problem is a standoff. If, as one scholar has noted, the data in our modern cases not infrequently assume aspects as far above the understanding of the everyday citizen as modern science is beyond the science of the fourteenth century, then I submit that the chances are that it is also well above the understanding of the judge; and if, as the same scholar has said, the average jury in such a case is about as helpful as it would be in solving a problem in higher mathematics, in industrial finance, or in electrical engineering, then I submit that the average judge is not the proper stalwart to fill the breach.

And if, as Professor Leon Green opined, the mere voter can do the job no longer, but must stand by for one who knows more about the true interests of society, more about the determination of facts and more about handling the complex business of men, then I submit, the mere voter is no longer qualified to vote, but should stand by for one who knows more about the true interests of society. For ultimately, the fact determinations involved in voting for a mayor, a governor, a congressman, or a President are more complex and infinitely more significant than any fact determinations called for from the jury box. . . .

THE RÔLE OF A JURY IN A CIVIL CASE

A Canadian Queen's Counsel, well versed in trial techniques, defends the civil jury in positive terms. He asserts that through the jury justice is kept in touch with the people, continuing the administration of justice as a popular institution. This is done by keeping fact-finding in the administration of justice out of the clouds and by removing it from the ivory tower and by bringing more common sense into the decisions.

In discussing the role of a jury in a civil case many considerations inevitably arise.

The first of these may well be, should we retain the jury system in civil cases at all? To this question I think there can be no proper answer but a ringing affirmative.

The right to trial by jury is the heritage of our common law—it has served well for countless generations. In the perspective given us by history we can see it as an institution protecting our citizens against the harshness of outdated

W. S. Martin, "The Rôle of a Jury in a Civil Case," Jury Trials. Special Lectures of the Law Society of Upper Canada. *Toronto: Richard De Boo Ltd., 1959. Copyright 1959 by The Law Society of Upper Canada. Reprinted with permission of the copyright owner. Footnotes have been omitted.*

laws. The man in the street looks on the jury as a bulwark against injustice—that will protect him from the insolence of those in public office—will shield the weak against the strong.

The average man may well feel that a judge dwelling on the pastoral uplands of the law has lost the common touch, if indeed he ever had it. He will wonder if a judge hewing to the lines established by legal precedent will fully appreciate all the facts in his case.

His view of a jury is entirely different. He feels that the jury box contains twelve members of his community. He will know that their one desire is to see that justice, as they understand it, shall be done between the two people who have placed themselves unreservedly in their hands. They may be ignorant of the law but in their common wisdom they are fully aware of the dangers and tribulations of ordinary life. They are patient and generous to counsel who appear before them, but they resent bitterly anything which they think is a trick. They will tolerate no subterfuge.

They will listen for interminable periods to common sense but will become uneasy and restless under a barrage of ill-advised words. They will be annoyed at an ill-timed jest and they will detest the smallest attempt to bully a witness or themselves.

But as a tribunal for dispensing justice, the centuries have proved them to be without equal.

I know of no man in the history of the English speaking world who practised more extensively before juries than the famous English counsel, Sir Patrick Hastings. He had a practice extending over almost half a century during which he was on one side or the other of every important jury case in England.

At the close of his notable forensic career this is what he had to say about juries:

> *During all the years I have practised before them I hardly remember a single instance in which they were*

wrong in the decision which they gave. They have often been against me, and upon those occasions I have been properly annoyed, but upon thinking the case over, as I always did, in the end I have come to the conclusion that they were right. Their verdict may not have been strictly in accordance with that which we know as the law of evidence, but according to the law of justice and common sense there was no fault to be found with the decision at which they arrived. I am quite satisfied that in the end twelve ordinary English men and women sitting together form the best tribunal that civilization has yet devised and any legislator who seeks to curtail the activities of juries does a great disservice to the nation. In my view a jury is almost invariably right and I know of no judge of whom I could so wholeheartedly say the same.

We need search for no other or better authority and we can rest our case for the retention of the jury system based on the collective experience of the British public and the individual experience of one of her greatest advocates.

But there are other cogent reasons for the retention of the jury system in civil cases and I think we should look at a few of them together. A reason for the continuance of the jury system is that it prevents the Bar from becoming a priestly class. Sir William Holdsworth also demonstrates how quickly lawyers and judges can get away from community thinking and follow "law for law's sake" in an effort to build a monument of legal perfection.

But Sir William's erudition pales beside the graphic and savage illustrations by Charles Dickens in probably his best novel *Bleak House*.

The novel begins and ends in Chancery where, as you know, there are no juries. Its opening chapter describes the fog:

Fog everywhere. Fog up the river where it flows among green aits and meadows; fog down the river where it rolls defiled among the tiers of shipping and the waterside pollutions of a great and dirty city—fog on the Essex marshes—fog on the Kentish heights.

. . . And hard by Temple Bar, in Lincoln's Inn Hall, at the very heart of the fog, sits the Lord High Chancellor in his High Court of Chancery.

Never can there come fog too thick, never can there come mud and mire too deep, to assort with the groping and floundering condition which this High Court of Chancery, most pestilent of hoary sinners, holds this day in the sight of heaven and earth.

Then Dickens tells us of the famed suit in Chancery.

Jarndyce and Jarndyce drones on. This scarecrow of a suit has in the course of time become so complicated that no man alive knows what it means. The parties to it understand it least; but it has been observed that no two Chancery lawyers can talk about it five minutes without coming to a total disagreement as to all the premises.

And then, at the end of the book, all available funds in the estate having been consumed in costs, this conversation takes place between one of the relatives and Mr. Kenge of Messrs. Kenge and Carboy.

[*Mr. Kenge*] *"You are to reflect, Mr. Woodcourt—Jarndyce and Jarndyce has been termed not inaptly a monument of Chancery practice—for many years—the —a—I would say the flower of the bar and the—a—I would presume to add the matured autumnal fruits of the woolsack have been lavished upon Jarndyce and Jarndyce."*

The relative then enquires: "Do I understand the whole estate is found to have been absorbed in costs?" And the answer was of course, "Yes."

In his introduction to *Bleak House* Mr. G. K. Chesterton says, "Dickens had a singularly just mind. He was wild in his caricatures but very sane in his impressions."

Earlier in his introduction Mr. Chesterton had said: "But he meant us to take the smokey atmosphere seriously. Charles Dickens who was, like all men who are really funny about funny things, horribly serious about serious things, certainly meant us to read the story of *Bleak House* in terms of his protest and his insurrection against the emptiness and arrogance of law, against the folly and the pride of judges."

So much for the argument that we could become a priestly class.

Lastly, the jury system should be retained to keep the people participating in the administration of justice. Our citizens through centuries have distrusted individual experts in the administration of their rights—and with good cause. Not only does power tend to corrupt but it tends to give those who wield it a contempt for the masses. Limitation of that power must be sought through politicians, which is an unsatisfactory process, or the circumstances which necessitate change must be allowed to degenerate into calamity. In the meantime, while awaiting the deluge, countless people suffer.

But the jury waits on no one. It is independent of politicians and outside influences. It brings to the decision of each case an approach fresh from the community and in that broad field of discretion arising from disputed facts it applies community standards. These are the standards by which the parties to the action live. Truly the jury guarantees that the law shall belong to the people.

* * *

IX

A COMPARISON OF JURY VERDICTS AND JUDGE DECISIONS

TRIAL BY JURY

A thoughtful law professor gathered facts which indicate revealing information about the jury attitude toward plaintiff and defendants, toward corporations and individuals, toward assessment of damage as compared with that of thoughtful judges.

My subject, as I understand it, deals with the practical utility of jury trials. The question which I am to discuss is this: Are there any advantages or disadvantages in jury trials as compared with court trials in respect to the final results obtained?

We all have general ideas upon that subject, but I think they are ordinarily based on very vague grounds. Those who are successful in jury trials are likely to consider their results more satisfactory than court trials, while those who do no trial work are perhaps less impressed with the jury as triers of facts. Lawyers sometimes approve or disapprove of trial by jury as the standard method of determining issues of fact, on the basis of isolated cases in their own ex-

Edson R. Sunderland, "Trial by Jury," 11 University of Cincinnati Law Review 120 (1937). *Footnotes have been omitted.*

perience which have made a strong impression upon their minds and have convinced them, perhaps without sufficient grounds, that jury trials do or do not produce better results than court trials. But generally speaking, I think no exact information has been available as to the differences in results, if any, between jury trials and court trials.

In an effort to secure some actual data in regard to such differences, I undertook not long ago to make a study of the judgments rendered after trial of issues in a sufficiently large number of cases to provide a reasonable statistical basis for comparison of the two types of trials. I investigated the records in a number of counties in Michigan, including Wayne County, where Detroit is located. I had the original files investigated in each case to determine: (1) the nature of the action, (2) the character of the parties involved in the action, (3) whether the case was tried by a jury or by the court, (4) who got the verdict, (5) its amount in case it was for the plaintiff, and (6) how long the trial lasted.

The counties that I studied were selected to give a cross-section of the state. In Wayne County, with a population of about 2,000,000, I had all the records examined for a period of six months. There were about 1,200 cases in that period in which judgments were rendered after trial by the court or by a jury.

I examined the records for about two years in Kent County, where Grand Rapids is located, a county with a population of 240,000. I examined the records for two years in Kalamazoo County, a smaller industrial county, and in three rural counties for a period of from 10 to 15 or 20 years, in order to get enough cases for statistical purposes.

The first question considered was: Do juries and judges differ in their distribution of verdicts as between plaintiff and defendant, and if so, how? I think one would expect that juries, who represent the attitude of the people, would be less conservative than the judges, who are supposed to represent the vested interests. Generally speaking, plaintiffs as a class are more likely to include people who do not have property, and defendants as a class are more likely to include those who do have property, because a plaintiff is not deterred from bringing suit by want of assets, while a defendant is unlikely to be sued if it is clear that the judgment cannot be collected. So that if juries are more affected than judges by notions of social justice, one would expect that plaintiffs would receive a larger percentage of verdicts in jury cases than in cases tried by the judges.

The situation seems slightly analogous to that in the justices' courts, where plaintiffs win so frequently. I had an examination made of all judgments rendered by justices of the peace in six typical counties in Michigan, and found that of 933 judgments rendered, 926 were for the plaintiff. That gave the plaintiffs 99.2 per cent of judgments and the defendants, 0.8 per cent.

While no one would expect juries to go as far as that, I thought a study of the cases might indicate a similar tendency on the part of juries to favor plaintiffs as against defendants. The results are as follows:

I classified the cases into those based on contract and those based on tort, in order to bring out the difference, if any, in this regard as between contract and tort cases. In Wayne County, out of 391 contract cases, I found that juries gave verdicts to the plaintiff in 76 per cent of the cases, and the court found for the plaintiff in 72 per cent of the cases. In 403 tort cases, where one would expect that juries would be more likely to favor plaintiffs, it appeared that juries gave the verdicts to the plaintiff in 64 per cent of the cases and the court found for the plaintiff in exactly the same percentage of cases—64 per cent. Combining all the contract and tort cases, it appeared that the plaintiff succeeded before the jury in 70 per cent of the cases, and succeeded before the court in 68 per cent of the cases. So small a difference was obviously negligible, so that the figures indicate that juries and courts took almost exactly the same attitude in regard to the distribution of verdicts between plaintiffs and defendants. The plaintiff had the same chance before the court as before the jury.

In the outlying counties the results were not quite the same. In all the cases examined, both in tort and in contract, the jury favored the plaintiff in 57 per cent while the court favored the plaintiff in 79 per cent. This discrepancy may be due to statistical variations resulting from the use of an insufficient number of cases.

The number studied was much larger in Wayne County and Detroit than in the outside counties, and I am inclined to think the Wayne figures give a more accurate picture. I conclude, therefore, on the basis of these statistics, that there can hardly be said to be any substantial difference in the attitude of juries and courts as between plaintiffs and defendants.

I may say that, in arriving at these figures, all cases were eliminated in which there was a corporation on one side and an individual on the other. I considered only those cases where there were corporations on both sides or individuals on both sides, so as to eliminate any question of prejudice as against a corporation and in favor of an individual. The conclusion stated is, therefore, based upon cases where there was no other element of party selection in awarding recoveries, so far as the records showed, than the mere difference between plaintiff and defendant.

The second question considered was: Do juries and judges differ in their distribution of verdicts as between individuals and corporations, when they are adversary parties? It has generally been supposed that juries are more likely than courts to favor individuals as against corporations. The results as to that question are as follows:

I selected all the cases where there was a corporation plaintiff and an individual defendant, and all the cases where there was an individual plaintiff and a corporation defendant, and then determined the percentage of verdicts which juries gave to individuals as against corporations and the percentage of verdicts which courts gave to individuals as against corporations. In Wayne County, where Detroit is located, it appeared that in contract cases juries favored the individual in 40 per cent of the cases while they favored the corporation in 60 per cent of the cases. The court favored the individual in 50 per cent of the cases and the corporation in 50 per cent. In tort cases, the juries reversed the distribution shown in the contract cases, finding for the individual in 61 per cent of the cases and for the corporation in 39 per cent, while the court preserved the equality shown in contract cases and sustained individuals in 51 per cent of the cases and corporations in 49 per cent of them. Combining all the cases, and there were a total of 381, which gives a fair basis for statistical treatment, I found that juries favored the individual in 53 per cent of the cases and the corporation in 47 per cent, while the court favored the individual in 50 per cent of the cases and the corporation in 50 per cent of them. It thus appears that juries favored individuals as against corporations in only 3 per cent more than half of the cases, which is a difference so slight as to have little significance, and the court showed no distinction whatever between them. It seems fair to conclude, therefore, that there is substantial identity in the attitude toward parties taken by courts and juries when deciding cases with individuals on one side and corporations on the other, and that there is nothing to be gained or lost by either an individual or a corporation through the use of a jury.

The third question was: Do judges and juries differ in their assessment of damages? Are juries more likely to assess larger damages than courts? For the purpose of determining that question, I divided the cases into various classes: contract, automobile accidents, railroad and streetcar accidents, other personal injuries, alienation of affections, fraud and deceit, assault and battery, false imprisonment, and other torts.

I found that in 443 contract cases in Wayne County in which the plaintiff won, the average jury verdict was $2,-224.00, while the average recovery from the court was $2,063.00. This average for court cases was obtained after excluding two abnormally large recoveries totalling about $600,000, which would have completely distorted the result.

In automobile accident cases, the average jury verdict was a little larger than the average court verdict, namely $2,736.00 as against $1,834.00. But in railroad and street car accident cases, this relation was reversed, the average jury verdict being $2,408.00, the average court verdict $3,-060.00.

In other personal injury cases, I found the two types of verdict almost identical. The average verdict of the jury was $2,138.00, while the average verdict from the court was $2,247.00.

In cases of alienation of affections, which is, perhaps, an illegitimate form of lawsuit in any event, the average verdict from the jury was $2,375.00, while the average from the court was $367.00.

In fraud and deceit cases the average jury verdict was $1,902.00; the average court verdict was $2,926.00.

In assault and battery and false imprisonment cases, which appeal to the emotions, the average jury verdict was $3,-805.00, and the court average was $812.00.

Taking all tort cases together, 353 in number, the average verdict from the jury was $2,323.00, and the average verdict from the court was $2,161.00.

Combining 796 cases of all kinds, both tort and contract, and eliminating the two very large recoveries already mentioned, the average jury verdict was $2,283.00, and the average court verdict was $2,110.00. In other words, there was no substantial difference in the assessment of damages as between courts and juries.

In the other counties outside of Wayne County there were 302 cases of all types in which the plaintiff won, and the average verdict rendered by the jury was $1,336.00, compared with an average recovery of $1,187.00 allowed by the court.

The conclusion which seems warranted by these figures is that both in metropolitan communities and in rural communities, juries and courts take essentially the same view as to assessment of damages, and except in such appeals to emotion as are inherent in cases of alienation of affections and assault and battery, neither the plaintiff nor the defendant secures any advantage in respect to the amount of the recovery by demanding a jury.

* * *

X

THE FUNCTION OF THE JURY

THE FUNCTIONS OF JURORS

One of America's most distinguished judges, lawyers, and law teachers has detailed the function of the jury and placed it in the perspective of the whole trial process.

The jury is undoubtedly the institution that most distinguishes trials at common law from trials under the Roman law, where a jury was unknown. It is only in those portions of our law that were imported from the Continent—equity, probate, and admiralty matters that followed in large degree the civil procedure of the Continent—that a jury is not used. It is the jury that gives English and American trials their distinctive characteristics.

As a substitute for the earlier modes of trial—trial by ordeal, trial by battle, and wager of law—trial by jury was as daring an innovation as has ever been attempted in the history of the common law. The origin of the jury may be traced back to the ninth century and the usages of the Carolingian monarchs from whom it was taken over by the Normans and thence transferred to England. The English

Arthur T. Vanderbilt, Judges and Jurors: Their Functions, Qualifications, and Selection. *Boston: Boston University Press, 1956. Copyright 1956 by the Trustees of Boston University. Reprinted with permission of the copyright owner. Footnotes have been omitted.*

gradually developed it as a mode of trial which first was made available in the royal common law courts alone for certain types of action; indeed, this more rational mode of trial was one of the prime reasons for the growing popularity of the royal courts.

The jury was originally a group of neighbors whose testimony was solicited as to their knowledge of the facts of an occurrence or of the ownership or possession of land. As dwellers in the locality, the jurors on the basis of personal information would give the answers as to such matters. "They are not judges . . . their function is . . . 'to recognize, to speak the truth.' " Not all residents of the vicinity were eligible as jurors, but from the first a property qualification was insisted upon. By the thirteenth century trial by jury was used in all criminal cases to determine the question of guilt or innocence and gradually trial by jury was extended to almost every kind of civil action. And by 1600 the jury was the usual mode of trial in the common law courts in all cases except for some of the extraordinary legal remedies such as certiorari, mandamus, and the like. Although at that time their character as witnesses basing their verdict on their own knowledge of the facts was not completely forgotten, testimony was being presented to the jurors for their consideration in deciding the issues. It was not for more than another century that it became established that the jurors, instead of giving a verdict based on their own knowledge, were to form an impartial body, having no opinion as to the case at issue and limited to deciding the case on the basis of the evidence presented in court.

* * *

The trial jury likewise became in some degree a shield in the trial of both civil and criminal cases not only against the harsh rules of the early common law but also against the more than occasional overbearing or subservient judge, for, as we have seen, up to the time of the Act of Settlement of 1701, judges merely served at the king's pleasure instead of during good behavior and a litigant had to fear that a judge might be more responsive to the royal will rather than to justice. Since at common law the jurors all had to agree to a verdict, a single juror might and often has mitigated the strict operation of the common law or some statute. On the other hand, it may be added, a single juror may and often has obstructed justice.

At first the only recourse against the verdict of a trial jury was by the verdict of another jury—a jury of twenty-four—that the first had perjured itself. This remedy, the writ of attaint, which developed while the jurors were still considered as witnesses rather than judges of the facts, resulted in the reversal of the first verdict and the imposition of very severe penalties on the original jury. The difficulties in obtaining a second verdict and the gradual change in the character of the jury made the remedy less effective. The Tudors and Stuarts employed the Council and Star Chamber to exercise pressure on juries by punishing them for corruption or false verdicts, and verdicts contrary to the Star Chamber's view of the evidence were likely to be considered corrupt or false.

It was not until 1670 in the famous *Bushell's Case* that jurors were really rendered free to determine their verdict without liability even if contrary to the court's direction. *Bushell's Case* did for the jury what the Act of Settlement at a later date, as we have seen, did for the judges—it gave them independence. This decision concerned the jurors who had acquitted two Quakers (one of them William Penn) in spite of the court's having attempted to extract a different verdict by keeping them without meat and drink for three days. For their conduct the jurors were fined and imprisoned. On a writ of habeas corpus they were discharged, Chief Justice Vaughan rendering a notable opinion in which he distinguished between the ministerial acts and the judicial acts of the jury; "the verdict itself, when given, is not an act ministerial but judicial, and according to the best of their judgment, for which they are not finable nor to be punished, but by attaint." The court reasoned that the jury are the judges of the facts. If a judge can order the jury on pain of punishment to take his view of the facts, what is the use of the jury? As the jury are judges of the facts, a disagreement with the judge as to the findings of fact cannot be penal:

> *Without a fact agreed, it is as impossible for a Judge, or any other, to know the law relating to that fact, or direct concerning it, as to know an accident that hath no subject.*
>
> *Hence it follows, that the Judge can never direct what the law is in any matter controverted, without first knowing the fact; and then it follows, that without his previous knowledge of the fact, the jury cannot go against his direction in law, for he could not direct. . . .*
>
> *But upon all general issues . . . (the jury) find for the plaintiff or defendant upon the issue to be tryed, wherein they resolve both law and fact complicately, and not the fact by itself; so though they answer not singly to the question what is the law, yet they determine the law in all matters where issue is joyn'd and tryed in the principal case, but where the verdict is special.*

Gradually attaint for a false verdict fell into disuse. As juries could no longer be penalized for finding a verdict contrary to judicial direction, the only way in which the crown could exert pressure was by controlling the choice of the jury, a practice which the Stuarts did not hesitate to exercise. Such evil practices, however, came to an end with the Revolution. The legitimate way of controlling erroneous verdicts came to be by an order, after a hearing, setting aside the verdict and directing a new trial.

The function of the jurors from the first was confined to dealing with facts. Questions of law were for the court. This division of responsibility between the judge and the jury did much to determine the nature of the pleadings at common law, molded the rules of evidence, and influenced trial procedure generally. Inasmuch as the jury were laymen, not versed in court procedure, the essential aim of common-law pleadings, in which the parties to a suit stated alternately their rival contentions, was to bring the pleadings to a point where the respective parties took opposite positions on some relevant question of law or fact. If they disagreed on a question of law, the court would dispose of the question of law on a demurrer. But if they disagreed on a relevant question of fact, an issue of fact was raised for a trial by jury. The great objective in a jury trial was thus the determination of a *single* question of fact. In this way it was hoped, and with a considerable measure of success, to submit to the jury an issue which was simple and entirely within their competence and to prevent misleading contentions on a variety of matters from beclouding their thinking. Even with these limitations it was deemed essential that the jury work under the supervision of the trial judge, who was to confine the activities of counsel to its proper sphere. The trial judge would prevent counsel from straying beyond the proper bounds of the case in their respective opening addresses to the jury, in offering documents and in presenting the oral testimony of witnesses by appropriate rulings of law, when objections were raised by counsel, on the evidence and by his concluding charge on the law to the jury. At common law the judge might question the witnesses where necessary in his opinion to bring out all the truth, and in delivering his charge he might analyze the evidence, summarize it and comment on it so long as he made it very clear that the resolution of the issue of the fact is exclusively the province of the jury.

* * *

The essential elements of the common law trial by jury embodied in the federal constitution have been recognized to be: "(1) that the jury should consist of twelve men, neither more nor less; (2) that the trial should be in the presence and under the superintendence of a judge having power to instruct them as to the law and advise them in respect of the facts; and (3) that the verdict should be unanimous. . . ." The occurrences in the jury room are secret in the sense that no one other than a member of the jury may be present during its deliberations and a juror may not be compelled to testify to what happened therein. If, however, it is first shown that a juror in some way was disqualified from serving as a juror, the other jurors may give testimony in corroboration of such facts.

We too often think of juries solely from the point of view of the litigants. It is interesting to have the view of a French judge who has written more understandingly of this country than has any other foreigner. Said Alexis de Tocqueville:

> *I do not know whether the jury is useful to those who have law suits; but I am certain it is highly beneficial to those who judge them; and I look upon it as one of the most efficacious means for the education of the people which society can employ.*

The jury is beneficial to the judge for at least two reasons. First of all, the facts of a case, both at the trial and appellate levels, are often more difficult to decide than the law of the case. Secondly and far more important, it spares him from making the harsh decisions that the sharp application of the law to the actual facts of a hard case would often require. While on the one hand in some cases juries may flaunt the law, in many cases juries effect equity. That basically was why the American colonists complained in the Declaration of Independence of the king "depriving us in many cases of the benefits of trial by jury," referring particularly to the establishment in the colonies of admiralty courts. Had the cases arising under the English trade acts been tried in the ordinary courts with a jury, probably there would have been no convictions. Accordingly, the colonists felt aggrieved and much of this predilection for jury decision was to persist through the nineteenth century.

* * *

The problem of the juror's function today has various facets. The question of the demarcation of questions of fact for jury's decision from the question of law for judicial decision continues to cause trouble because of the many instances where the decisions of questions of fact necessarily have legal connotations. In one view the basic problem is to so control the jury as to limit it to its function of deciding issues of fact. In the view of many the special verdict and special interrogatories are useful devices to serve this purpose. On the other hand there are others who testify to the value of the jury as an expression of community opinion. Despite the general acceptance of the proposition that questions of law are for the court and questions of fact only are for the jury, the jury's power to decide the whole case by a general verdict, frequently without the guidance of the judge to decide issues of law, is the crux of the dispute. The conflict is between those, on the one hand, who would limit the freedom of the jury by proper instructions by the judge, his comments on the evidence, use of his power to withdraw the case from the jury when the evidence is insufficient, as well as by devices such as the special verdict, and those, on the other hand, who regard this freedom of the jury to decide the law in some cases in the guise of a general verdict as a welcome power. It is said by the latter that "Traditionally juries are the devices by which the rigor of the law is modified pending the enactment of new statutes." Others are more critical of the jury making "its own 'law' in each case with little or no knowledge of, or reference to, what has been done before or regard to what will be done thereafter in similar cases." In such view prejudice is "the thirteenth juror."

Although the jury is used to a decreasing extent even in the United States, the constitutional guarantees of trial by jury insure that so long as the parties so desire they shall have the jury to which they are entitled. Trial by jury is a vital feature of judicial administration in this country, but the jury's lack of information as to the law and its lack of experience in weighing the probative force of testimony make the assistance and guidance of the judge whose only aim is to see that justice is done most essential. Since the judge may set aside a verdict and grant a new trial if the jury's verdict is opposed to the evidence, and may direct a verdict if there is no evidence to support any but one verdict, it is only logical that the jury be guided by the judge's analysis, summary, and comments on the evidence. The importance of a proper allocation of powers and functions between the judge and the jury is essential to the continued and proper employment of the trial jury.

XI

HISTORY OF THE JURY

VARIOUS THEORIES RESPECTING THE ORIGIN OF THE JURY

The history of the civil jury is difficult to trace and disputed by many people. Mr. Forsyth's thesis that it gradually arose from earlier methods of trial of the Anglo-Saxons and Anglo-Normans involving citizen participation in the decision-making process as a means of ensuring justice is widely accepted.

The rise and growth of the Jury system is a subject which ought to interest not only the lawyer but all who value the institutions of England, of which this is one of the most remarkable, being until recently a distinctive feature of our jurisprudence.

In the following pages an attempt is made to investigate its origin and trace its history, until it assumed the well-defined form and office with which we are so familiar, but which long excited the admiration and envy of the nations of Europe, until at last, by slow degrees and to a partial extent, many of them have succeeded in adopting it them-

William Forsyth, History of Trial by Jury. *(New Edition, James Appleton Morgan) New York: James Cockcroft & Company, 1875. Footnotes have been omitted.*

selves. The inquiry is more difficult than may at first sight appear. Trial by Jury does not owe its existence to any positive law:—it is not the creature of an Act of Parliament establishing the form and defining the functions of the new tribunal. It arose, as I hope to show, silently and gradually, out of the usages of a state of society which has forever passed away, but of which it is necessary to have a clear idea, in order to understand how this mode of trial first came into existence.

Few subjects have exercised the ingenuity and baffled the research of the historian more than the origin of the jury. No long time has elapsed since the popular opinion was—and perhaps it even now prevails—that it was an institution established by Alfred the Great; and we prided ourselves on the idea that this was one of the legacies of freedom bequeathed to us by our Anglo-Saxon ancestors. An enlightened spirit of historical criticism applied to the subject has, however, of late years done much to dissipate this delusion; and it would be unjust not to acknowledge how greatly in this country we are indebted for more correct views to the labors of Reeves, Palgrave, Starkie, and Hallam. But the jurists of Germany also deserve the praise of having investigated the question with profound learning and searching accuracy, and the frequent reference made in the course of this treatise to their works will prove how fully I appreciate the services they have rendered in the elucidation of the present inquiry.

Numerous have been the theories as to the birth and parentage of this the favorite child of the English law. Some writers have thought the origin so lost in the darkness of antiquity, as to render investigation hopeless. Thus Bourguignon says, "Its origin is lost in the night of time"; and the late Chief Commissioner Adam declares that "in England it is of a tradition so high that nothing is known of its origin; and of a perfection so absolute that it has remained in unabated rigor from its commencement to the present time."

Spelman was uncertain whether to attribute the origin of the system to the Saxons or the Normans. Du Cange and Hickes ascribed its introduction to the Normans, who themselves borrowed the idea from the Goths. Blackstone calls it "a trial that hath been used time out of mind in this nation, and seems to have been coeval with the first civil government thereof"; and he adds, "that certain it is that juries were in use among the earliest Saxon colonies." In his learned work on "The Origin and Progress of the Judicial Institutions of Europe," Meyer regards the jury as partly a modification of the Grand Assize established by Henry II, and partly an imitation of the feudal courts erected in Palestine by the Crusaders; and he fixes upon the reign of Henry III as the era of its introduction into England. The theory of Reeves in his "History of the Engish Law" is, that when Rollo led his followers into Normandy they carried with them this mode of trial from the North. He says that it was used in Normandy in all cases of small importance, and that when the Normans had transplanted themselves into England they endeavored to substitute it in the place of the Saxon tribunals. He speaks of it therefore as a novelty introduced by them soon after the Conquest, and says that it may be laid down with safety that the system did not exist in Anglo-Saxon times. Turner, on the other hand, in his "History of the Anglo-Saxons," thinks that it was then in use, "although no record marks the date of its commencement"; and he ought to have added, or "notices the fact of its existence." Sir Francis Palgrave says that a tribunal of sworn witnesses elected out of the popular courts and employed for the decision of rights of property may be traced to the Anglo-Saxon period; but that in criminal cases the jury appears to have been unknown until enacted by the Conqueror.

The opinion of one of the latest and ablest of our legal writers, Mr. Sergeant Stephen, seems to coincide with that of Reeves, for he says, "The most probable theory seems to be that we owe the germ of this (as of so many of our institutions) to the Normans, and that it was derived by them from Scandinavian tribunals, where the judicial number of twelve was always held in great veneration." He refers also to the Grand Coustumier as justifying the idea that the jury is of Norman origin. But we may remark in passing, that this work was written later than the year 1215, so that whatever may be the similarity of usage between the two countries which we find therein mentioned, it is more probable that the Norman was derived from the English.

Some writers, especially amongst the Germans, attribute the origin of the English Jury to a national recognition of the principle that no man ought to be condemned except by the voice of his fellow-citizens. And as the ancient courts of justice amongst the Teutonic nations were nothing more than assemblies of freemen, met together for the purpose of deliberating on whatever affected the interests of the gau or district of which they were the inhabitants, including the punishment of offenses and the settlement of civil claims, it has been thought that here is to be found the assertion of the same principle as pervades the jury-trial, and that therefore the latter is derived from and only a modification of the former.

But if this be so, how can we account for the fact that in England alone the system was developed into its modern form, and that while amidst all the freedom of Anglo-Saxon institutions it was unknown, it first assumed a distinct and historical character under the reign of a Norman king? We shall see, unless I am mistaken, in the course of our inquiry, that the jury does not owe its existence to any preconceived theory of jurisprudence, but that it gradually grew out of forms previously in use, and was composed of elements long familiar to the people of this country. Where such diversity of opinion prevails, and so many learned men have professed their inability to pierce the darkness that surrounds the early history of the subject, it well becomes a writer to be diffident of his own view; but I cannot help feeling persuaded that the rise of the jury system may be traced as a gradual and natural sequence from the modes of trial in use amongst the Anglo-Saxons and Anglo-Normans—that is, both before and after the Conquest—and that therefore in order to understand how it arose, we have only to make ourselves fully acquainted with those modes of trial and the state of society on which they so intimately depended. . . .

In endeavoring to trace the origin of any institution which has come down to us from remote antiquity, we must carefully consider under what aspect it appears when first noticed by contemporary writers. This often differs widely from the form and character which it acquires in the slow growth of years, and yet its identity may be proved with as much certainty as that of the river whose wellhead is a spring oozing out of a grassy bed, and which swells into a broad expanse of waters before it loses itself in the ocean. We shall only be deceived if we fix our attention upon its maturity rather than its infancy; upon its end rather than its beginning. In constitutional history this is eminently true. We must deal with institutions as philology does with words. To ascertain the derivation of the latter we resolve them into their earliest known forms, and these are often the only clue whereby we can discover the stock from which they sprung, and the meaning they primarily bore.

So in the case of Trial by Jury we must determine the point of time when it is first mentioned as an historical fact, and see what were then its characteristic features. We must know its primitive form, and observe in what point of view it was looked upon by the writers of the early ages. The subsequent changes it has undergone will not throw much light upon its origin—nay, they rather tend to mislead us by suggesting false analogies and wrong points of comparison; and many a specious but mistaken theory on the subject would have been avoided, if due attention had been paid to the accounts of the true nature of the tribunal which we find in the pages of Glanvill and Bracton, and of which we find incidental notice in contemporary annals and records.

Again, we must be careful not to attach too much importance to seeming analogies, or mistake partial resemblances for complete identity. It is this which has led so many writers to espouse conflicting views respecting the origin of the jury. By fixing their attention on particular points of two systems, and finding that these in a great measure correspond, they have imagined that the one must have been copied from the other. Thus some think that they discover the archetype of the jury in the Teutonic and Saxon compurgators, who were generally twelve in number, and whose oaths were conclusive of the matter in dispute. Others derive it from the Rachinburgen or Scabini of the continental nations; others from the sectatores and pares of the ancient county and feudal courts in this country.

One important feature of the institution is by no means peculiar to it. I mean the fact that it is a sworn tribunal—that its members decide under the solemn sanction of an oath. This was the case with the Dicasts at Athens and the Judices at Rome, and the same principle prevailed in the old Norse THING and German MALLUM, when the right of all the inhabitants of the gau or mark to be present at the judicial proceedings of these periodical assemblies became in practice limited to a few, as the representatives of the community.

But sufficient attention has not been paid to what is the distinctive characteristic of the system; namely, that the Jury consists of a body of men taken from the community at large, summoned to find the truth of disputed facts, who are quite distinct from the judges or court. Their office is to decide upon the effect of evidence, and thus inform the court truly upon the question at issue, in order that the latter may be enabled to pronounce a right judgment. But they are not the court itself, nor do they form part of it; and they have nothing to do with the sentence which follows the delivery of their verdict. Moreover, they are not members of any class or corporation, on whom, as distinct from the rest of their fellow-citizens, is imposed the task of taking part in judicial inquiries. They are called upon to serve as the particular occasion arises, and then return to their usual avocations and pursuits, so as to be absolutely free from any professional bias or prejudice.

Few writers, when speculating on the rise of the jury, have kept this principle of its being separate from the court and employed solely to determine questions of fact, steadily in view. They have generally confounded the jurors with the court, and have thus imagined an identity between the former and those ancient tribunals of Europe where a select number of persons—often twelve—were taken from the community and appointed to try causes, but who did so in the capacity of judges, and when satisfied of the evidence awarded and pronounced the doom.

These are the Geschwornen-Gerichte to which the jurists of Germany of late years have been so fond of appealing, as the model upon which they wish to reform their modern courts of judicature, and which they assume to have been in principle the same as the English Jury.

But a little reflection will convince us that this is not so, and that the distinction above insisted on is not a mere formal one, but of a radical and important kind. It involves, in fact, the question of the possibility of the tribunal continuing to exist. A court of justice where the whole judicial authority is vested in persons taken from time to time from amongst the people at large, with no other qualification required than that of good character, can only be tolerated in a state of society of the most simple kind. As the affairs of civil life become more complicated, and laws more intricate and multiplied, it is plainly impossible that such persons, by whatever name they are called, whether judges or jurors, can be competent to deal with legal questions. The law becomes a science which requires laborious study to comprehend it; and without a body of men trained to the task, and capable of applying it, the rights of all would be set afloat —tossed on a wide sea of arbitrary, fluctuating, and contradictory decisions. Hence in all such popular courts as we are describing, it has been found necessary to appoint jurisconsults to assist with their advice, in matters of law, the uninstructed judges. These at first acted only as assessors, but gradually attracted to themselves and monopolized the whole judicial functions of the court. There being no machinery for keeping separate questions of law from questions of fact, the lay members felt themselves more and more inadequate to adjudge the causes that came before them. They were obliged perpetually to refer to the legal functionary who presided, and the more his authority was enhanced, the more the power of the other members of the court was weakened, and their importance lessened, until it was seen that their attendance might without sensible inconvenience be dispensed with altogether. And of course this change was favored by the crown, as it thereby gained the important object of being able, by means of creatures of its own, to dispose of the lives and liberties of its subjects under the guise of legal forms. Hence there arose in Europe, upon the ruins of the old popular tribunals, the system of single judges appointed by the king and deciding all matters of fact and law, and it brought with it its odious train of secret process and inquisitorial examinations. But the result was inevitable. The ancient courts of Scandinavia and Germany carried in their very constitution the element of their own destruction, and this consisted in the fact that the whole judicial power was in the hands of persons who had no special qualifications for their office.

Far otherwise has been the case in England. Here the jury never usurped the functions of the judge. They were originally called in to aid the court with information upon questions of fact, in order that the law might be properly applied; and this has continued to be their province to the present day. The utility of such an office is felt in the most refined as well as in the simplest state of jurisprudence. Twelve men of average understanding are at least as competent now as they were in the days of Henry II to determine whether there is sufficient evidence to satisfy them that a murder has been committed, and that the party charged with the crime is guilty. The increased technicality of the law does not affect their fitness to decide on the effect of proofs. Hence it is that the English jury flourishes still in all its pristine vigor, while what are improperly called the old juries of the continent have either sunk into decay or been totally abolished.

A near approximation indeed to the proper functions of the jury is to be found in the proceedings of criminal state trials amongst the ancient Romans, although we may be quite certain that the English institution is in no way copied from them. There we find a presiding judge, who was either the prætor or a judex quæstionis specially appointed by him, and a body of judices taken from a particular class, at one time the equestrian, and at another the senatorial, whose duty it was to determine the fact of the guilt or innocence of the accused. At the close of the evidence they were said to be missi in consilium by the judge, that is, told "to consider their verdict," and to each were given three tablets marked respectively with the letters A. for Absolvo, C. for Condemno, and N. L. for Non Liquet, one of which he threw into an urn, and the result of the trial was determined by the majority of the letters that appeared. If the fatal C. prevailed, the prætor pronounced the sentence, with which the judices did not interfere. So far the course of procedure seems closely analogous to our own. But the important difference is this. The Roman judices might, without any breach of legal duty, acquit in spite of the most conclusive evidence of guilt; for they were entitled as representing the sovereign people to exercise the prerogative of mercy, and their verdict in that case implied and was equivalent to a pardon. Their functions therefore were not, like those of the jurymen of later times, restricted to the mere finding of facts, but extended to the exercise of a power which, with us, is lodged in the supreme executive of the state. We may further add, that when the prætor announced the verdict of the majority, if it was condemno he used the words Videtur Fecisse or Non Jure Videtur Fecisse; if it was absolvo, the words Non Videtur Fecisse, or Jure Videtur Fecisse; and perhaps the last form was adopted not only when the facts had been proved against the accused, and there was a legal excuse for the deed, but also when the prætor saw that the acquittal was intended as an act of mercy and a pardon.

I believe it to be capable almost of demonstration, that the English jury is of indigenous growth, and was not copied or borrowed from any of the tribunals that existed on the continent. In order to prove this, it will be necessary to examine what those tribunals in ancient times really were, and show wherein the difference between them and our own system consisted; a difference, in my opinion, of so essential a kind, that writers never could have been so misled as to confound them, if they had not occupied themselves rather with what the jury now is—namely, the sole judge of the effect of evidence produced, and the arbiter of compensation for contracts broken and injuries received—than with what it originally was, when its verdict was nothing more than the conjoint testimony of a fixed number of persons deposing to facts within their own knowledge. . . .

THE JURY SYSTEM IN AMERICA: GUARANTEES OF FEDERAL AND STATE CONSTITUTIONS

In the United States written constitutions have played a part in the development and preservation of the right to jury trial. The impact of constitutional provisions is described by Mr. Busch.

Jury trials in Colonial America. When the colonization of America began, the jury system (grand and petit) was an established institution in England which had practically superseded the older methods of trial of criminal and common law cases. The colonial grants were made at various times over a period of one hundred and twenty-five years. They were made by different monarchs for widely variant purposes. The vast territories allotted the respective grantees, extending from Maine to Georgia, presented a diversity of physical conditions which called for particular adjustments. In their essential character, and especially in their religious backgrounds, the several settlements presented striking contrasts. The royal grants differed widely in their terms. Connecticut and Rhode Island were chartered colonies with extensive rights of self-government; except for the reserved right of the Crown to intervene in such exceptional cases as were deemed calculated to affect foreign relations or essential royal prerogatives, these colonies were subject only to such restrictions as the Crown or Parliament might impose generally upon all English colonies. In Maryland and Pennsylvania broad powers were vested in proprietors whose rule, subject to rarely exercised royal veto, was absolute. The original royal patents or grants to Carolina, Virginia, Massachusetts, and New Hampshire were subsequently declared forfeited, or, as in the case of Georgia, expired by limitation, and these, together with New York, part of Delaware, and most of New Jersey (acquired from the Dutch) became royal provinces. These were administered by a governor, council, and executive officers nominated by the Crown, and a representative assembly elected by the freeholders among the colonists. All of the colonies enjoyed a broad measure of home rule in purely domestic affairs. The local courts, whether constituted by charter, executive order, or legislative act, followed the English pattern. The same was true of judicial procedures, and the use of an accusing or grand jury and a petit or traverse jury existed in all of the colonies. Due, however, to the diversities in their character, purpose, and control and their remoteness one from another, we find at the end of the colonial period pronounced differences in the extent of the application of the jury trial to various types of cases, and local peculiarities in the institution itself. The essential fact is that in 1776 the jury system was an established colonial institution in both civil and criminal cases, and was esteemed a valuable right.

Provisions of state constitutions before the adoption of the Federal Constitution. State constitutions were adopted by Virginia, Pennsylvania, Delaware, Maryland, Connecticut, New Hampshire, New Jersey, and North Carolina in 1776, by New York, Georgia, and Vermont in 1777, by South Carolina in 1778, and by Massachusetts in 1780. In several instances the so called constitutions were hurried expressions of the local congresses, enacted pursuant to the recommendation of the Continental Congress (May 15, 1776) that "the respective assemblies and conventions of the United States, where no government sufficient to the exigencies of their affairs hath been hitherto established, * * * adopt such government, as may, in the opinion of the representatives of the people, best conduce to the happiness and safety of their constituents." Connecticut, by an act of its legislature, continued the charter of 1662 in force as "the civil constitution of this state under the sole authority of the people thereof independent of any king or prince whatsoever." In New Hampshire, the declaration of its congress recited that the royal governor had fled "leaving it destitute of legislature or courts to punish offenders" and provided for a council of twelve to carry on a civil government. Rhode Island took no action whatever, and until 1842 operated under its royal charter of 1663. The constitutional enactments of the other colonies contained express or implied reference to the right of trial by jury, and provided for its continuance. In the cases of Virginia, Pennsylvania, Maryland, New Jersey, North Carolina, South Carolina, New

York, Georgia, Vermont, and Massachusetts, the reference to trial by jury is specific. The Constitution of Delaware provided that the common law of England, as well as so much of the statute law as had been theretofore adopted in practice in the state, should remain in full force, unless thereafter altered by the legislature; the later Constitution of 1792 expressly guaranteed the right of trial by jury. The value put upon the right of trial by jury is emphasized in a number of the constitutions. Thus, in the first Constitution of New Jersey it is declared that "the inestimable right of trial by jury shall remain confirmed as a part of the law of this colony, without repeal, forever." The Constitution of North Carolina declared "the ancient mode of trial by jury is one of the best securities of the rights of the people, and should remain secure and inviolable." The Constitution of Massachusetts (1780), after providing that no person could be arrested, imprisoned, despoiled, or deprived of his property, immunities, or privileges; put out of the protection of the law; exiled or deprived of his life, liberty, or estate but by the judgment of his peers or the law of the land, added "in criminal prosecutions the verification of the facts in the vicinity where they happen is one of the greatest securities of the life, liberty, and property of the citizen."

This brief reference to the constitutions of the several colonies, which were adopted before the Federal Constitutional Convention of 1789, is pertinent not only as showing the hold which the jury system had taken upon the colonies, but also as serving to explain the bitter controversy which followed the promulgation of the original draft of the Federal Constitution because it contained no specific reference to the preservation of the right of trial by jury in civil cases.

Provisions of the submitted draft of the Federal Constitution concerning juries and jury trials. The draft of the Federal Constitution, as submitted to the various state legislatures for approval, contained but one section (Art. III, Sec. 2, Clause 3) relating to juries. That section provided:

"The trial of all crimes, except in cases of impeachment, shall be by jury; and such trial shall be held in the state where the said crimes shall have been committed; but when not committed within any state, trial shall be at such place or places as the Congress may by law have directed." There was no provision in the draft for a grand jury or for jury trials in civil cases.

Opposition to the submitted draft. These omissions precipitated one of the bitterest attacks that was made upon the draft. Thomas Jefferson and Patrick Henry were prominent in the opposition. Jefferson's criticism was general, i.e., that the draft contained no "bill of rights." He repeatedly stressed the inadequacy of the document as respected trial by jury. In a letter to Madison he proposed an amendment providing for "trial by juries in all matters of fact triable by the law of the land." Jefferson continued his opposition to the Constitution until it was adopted by Massachusetts with definite instructions to her delegates in Congress to insist upon the bill of rights (the first ten amendments) which had then been drafted. Justice Story, writing at a later period, expressed the universal sentiment of the colonies. "It [the seventh amendment] is a most important and valuable amendment and places upon the high ground of constitutional right the inestimable privilege of trial by jury in civil cases—a privilege scarcely inferior to that in criminal cases, which is conceded by all to be essential to political and civil liberty."

Hamilton, in one of the Federalist papers (No. 88) vainly attempted to answer this storm of criticism. He ridiculed the contention that by legal construction the reference in the draft to the right of trial by jury in criminal cases implied its abolition in civil cases; on the contrary, he contended that all state institutions, including the institution of the jury in civil cases, would be uninfluenced by the adoption of the Federal Constitution. He further asserted that it was impossible to draft a simple, general provision for jury trials in civil cases which could be made applicable to all of the states, because of an irreconcilable diversity in the use of juries in the several states. Specifically, he pointed out that some of the states—New Jersey, New York, Virginia, Maryland, and South Carolina—allowed jury trials in common law cases only and then with important exceptions, while in others—Pennsylvania, Delaware, and North Carolina—the distinction between common law and equity was not clearly recognized, and the practice of jury trials extended beyond strictly common law cases; also, that in Connecticut, Rhode Island, Massachusetts, and New Hampshire juries were more extensively used than in any of the other states. He further called attention to the peculiar practices of certain states which permitted an appeal from an adverse verdict of one jury to another "special jury" (Georgia), and from one jury to another (in the "four Eastern states") until one side or the other had obtained two out of three verdicts. Hamilton's final answer to the criticism, and quite obviously the one representing his basic view, was that while trial by jury in criminal cases materially concerns the security of liberty, he "could not readily discern the inseparable connection between the existence of liberty and trial by jury in civil cases: that there were many civil cases in which trial by jury was not the best method of procedure," and the choice of procedure ought to be left to the individual states.

As already observed, Hamilton's efforts were futile to prevent amendments to the draft in the nature of a bill of rights, which included further specific guaranties in criminal cases, and expressly provided for trial by jury in civil cases.

The fifth, sixth, and seventh amendments.—The fifth and sixth amendments amplified the constitutional provisions respecting crimes and criminal prosecutions. The fifth amendment provided that "No person shall be held to answer for a capital or otherwise infamous crime unless on a presentment or indictment of a grand jury except in cases arising in the land or naval forces, or in the militia, when in actual service in time of war or public danger."

The sixth amendment provided that "In all criminal prosecutions, the accused shall enjoy the right to a speedy and public trial, by an impartial jury of the State and district wherein the crime shall have been committed."

The seventh amendment, applicable to civil cases, provided that "In suits at common law, where the value in controversy shall exceed twenty dollars, the right of trial by jury shall be preserved; and no fact tried by a jury shall be otherwise re-examined in any court of the United States than according to the rules of the common law."

Provisions of Federal Constitution and amendments applicable only to cases properly cognizable by the Federal courts. The provisions of Art. III, Sec. 2, Clause 3 of the Constitution, and the fifth, sixth, and seventh amendments respecting juries and trials by juries have been uniformly held to be restrictions upon the Federal Government and not upon the states.

Article III, Sec. 2, Clause 3. With specific reference to this clause, the Supreme Court has declared that the intent of the constitutional framers was to preserve the right of trial by jury for the protection of one accused of a Federal crime; that it was not their purpose to establish the jury for the trial of crimes as an integral and inseparable part of the court, but only as one of its instrumentalities. The sixth amendment amplifies this clause, but does not modify or conflict with it. The clause is not applicable to proceedings in the state courts.

This section has been construed as not applying to petty offenses, which were triable by common law or particular colonial law without a jury, or to petty offenses created by later law which are comparable in degree of infamy or prescribed punishment to offenses which at common law were triable without a jury. Specifically, it has been held that a defendant charged with violation of a statute prescribing a penalty of a fine and/or a jail sentence of not to exceed ninety days for failure to collect and account for a tax on a sale of an unused railroad ticket was not entitled to a jury trial; that one charged with contempt of court was not entitled to a jury trial; that refusal to testify before a military tribunal, where the penalty was $500 fine or six months' imprisonment, or both, was a petty offense triable without a jury. Similarly, as to a charge of soliciting prostitution, where the maximum punishment was a ninety day jail sentence; a charge of misbranding under the Pure Food and Drug Act, where the penalty was a fine only; and a charge of illegally selling liquor, where the penalty was a fine and a maximum sentence of two years in jail.

On the other hand, the section has been construed as entitling a defendant to a jury trial on a charge of violation of the excise laws where the penalty was a fine and imprisonment; on a charge of violation of the National Prohibition Act, where the penalty was a fine and twelve months in jail; and, on a charge of so recklessly driving an automobile as to endanger life or property, where the extreme penalty provided was imprisonment for not more than one year.

The Fifth Amendment. This amendment is a limitation upon the Federal Government and has no relation to state action. The purpose of the provision was to limit the powers of the Federal Legislature, as well as to prosecute officers of the United States. No declaration of Congress that a crime is infamous is needed to secure or is competent to defeat the constitutional safeguard. The Federal Courts, however, have defined an infamous crime, as the term is used in the amendment, as one in which the law authorizes the court to award an infamous punishment, such as imprisonment in the penitentiary. Counterfeiting, fraudulent altering of election poll books, fraudulent voting, embezzlement by an officer of a national bank, have been held to be infamous crimes. Conspiracy, which is punishable by fine or imprisonment is not deemed infamous and may be instituted by information. Attempting to influence a jury by written communications (18 U.S.C.A. 243), punishable by fine or imprisonment for not more than six months, has been held not to be an infamous crime. Aliens, as well as citizens, are protected by the amendment from prosecution for infamous crimes, unless on the presentment of a grand jury. The protection of the amendment does not extend to citizens or aliens who offend against the laws of war; such offenses are triable before a military commission without a jury.

The Sixth Amendment. This amendment limits the powers of the Federal Government only; it is not a restriction upon the states. The provision has been held applicable to criminal trials in the District of Columbia and the territories, but not to Puerto Rico, Hawaii, the Philippine Islands, the Canal Zone, and the Virgin Islands, because the latter have not been incorporated into the Union. Similarly, the provision is held not to apply to an American citizen before a Consular Tribunal, charged with an offense committed in a foreign country.

The Seventh Amendment. This amendment, preserving the right of jury trial in civil cases, applies only to courts sitting under the authority of the Federal Congress, including the courts of the territories and the District of Columbia. It does not apply to the courts of the several states, even where such courts are called upon to enforce rights created by Federal statutes. It does not operate to prevent a state from limiting the application, or altering the form of jury trial as it existed at the time of the adoption of the state's first constitution. A territorial statute, however, which attempts to alter the common law form of jury is void.

That part of the amendment which provides that no fact tried by a jury shall be otherwise reexamined in any court of the United States than according to the rules of the common law is treated in a later connection.

The Fourteenth Amendment. The provision of the fourteenth amendment that "No state shall . . . deprive any person of life, liberty, or property without due process of law" does not extend the provisions of the Constitution or its earlier amendments respecting jury trials to state judicial procedures. "Due process," as used in the fourteenth amendment, has been construed to mean "substantial accord with the law and usage in England before the Declaration of Independence, and in this country since it became a nation, in similar cases," and the regularly constituted judicial process indiscriminately employed in a particular state.

Provisions of state constitutions respecting juries. Reference has already been made to the express or implied provisions for jury trials in the first constitutions of the thirteen original states and Vermont.

The Ordinance for the Government of the Northwest Territory (1787) provided (Art. II): "The inhabitants of said territory shall always be entitled to the benefits of the writ of habeas corpus and trial by jury."

Broad general provisions respecting the right of trial by jury in both criminal and civil cases are contained in the constitutions of all the states except Louisiana. In the constitution of that state (1921) there is a specific guaranty of the right of trial by jury in criminal cases (Art. VII, Sec. 41), and the use of juries in civil cases is recognized in the provision (Art. VII, Sec. 42) that the legislature may provide for the drawing of jurors in both criminal and civil cases. In most of the constitutions, the language employed, following that used in the sixth amendment to the Federal Constitution, is that "in all criminal prosecutions the accused shall have the right to a speedy public trial by an impartial jury of the county or district in which the offense is alleged to have been committed," and, generally, that "the right of trial by jury shall remain inviolate," or "the right of trial by jury as heretofore enjoyed shall remain inviolate."

The constitutions of many of the states contain additional references to jury trials—providing for or authorizing the legislature to provide for waiver of jury trials in civil and criminal cases (other than capital), conditioning the right to a jury trial upon the seriousness of the offense or the amount in controversy, or a specific demand, permitting the use of fewer than twelve jurors in specified cases, and altering the ancient requirement of unanimity as a prerequisite to a lawful verdict.

XII

SELECTION OF JURORS

JURY SELECTION ANALYZED

The quality of jurors of course will affect the decisions of cases. How jurors are chosen, who may be excused, the standard of selection are carefully set out in this scholarly paper.

Jury selection may be described, at least tentatively, as an administrative procedure, conducted according to legislative rules and standards, subject to judicial review. The validity of this tentative description will be discussed after the proposed analysis has been made.

I. Legislative Rules and Standards

A. Qualifications for Jury Service

1. Service in General

(a) Physical capacity. In order to render efficient jury service, a juror should be able to see clearly, hear clearly, and speak with sufficient clarity to make himself understood. He should be able to attend court, and should be free from every bodily condition likely to impair the quality of his thinking. Beyond these simple requirements physical qualifications need not go. Statutes, however, have not stopped

William Wirt Blume, "Jury Selection Analyzed: Proposed Revision of Federal System," 42 Michigan Law Review *831 (1944). Copyright 1944 by Michigan Law Review. Reprinted with permission of the copyright holder. Footnotes have been omitted.*

here, but have required other physical qualities such as a minimum age, a specified sex, a particular color of skin. Being under a certain maximum age also has been required.

Age measured in years has reference to physical existence, and may or may not indicate the state of maturity of a person's mind. It is customary, however, to assume that persons under a certain minimum physical age are not mentally qualified to serve as jurors. But it is not proper to assume that persons over the minimum physical age have a corresponding mental age. It is also improper to assume that a person over a certain maximum age is either mentally, physically, or otherwise unfit for jury service. It may be proper to exempt the latter persons from jury service, but in doing so care ought to be taken not to give the intended exemption the effect of a disqualification.

An inference as to a person's physical, mental, or other capacity for jury service cannot properly be drawn from the mere fact of sex. Exemption of women engaged in bearing and rearing children is another matter.

It is likewise improper to draw an inference as to a person's capacity to serve as a juror from his race or from the color of his skin. Color may indicate social position, but, as noted below, social position is not a basis for jury service.

(b) Mental capacity. To serve as a juror a person should have at least average adult intelligence. Assuming that mental growth ceases at the age of fourteen, he should have a mental age of at least fourteen. Furthermore, this capacity should be constant. If at unpredictable times a person may lack full mental capacity he is not qualified for jury service.

In addition to ability to think clearly a juror should have certain knowledge, habits, and attitudes. More specifically, he should have a sufficient knowledge of human affairs to distinguish truth from error. By habit he should be cautious in reaching conclusions. In attitude he should be public-minded, that is to say, he should have an established sense of responsibility for the welfare of the community in which he serves. In attempts to prescribe these qualities statutes have provided that jurors must be "discreet," "judicious," "of sound mind and discretion," "of sound judgment," "intelligent," "well informed," "of fair education." A minimum physical age is prescribed in the hope that these qualities will be found in persons who reach that age.

Knowledge of the English language is specifically required. This qualification, however, is not related to intelligence or to education, but, like the requirements that a juror be able to hear and speak, has to do with ability to communicate with others.

(c) Moral character. Statutes commonly provide that jurors must be of "good moral character." More specifically, according to some statutes, jurors must be "temperate," "not habitual drunkards," "not professional gamblers," not convicted of certain crimes. The habits and other facts referred to are indicative of bad moral character. It should be noted, also, that habitual drunkards and drug addicts are likely to be lacking in mental and physical capacity at unpredictable periods of time.

(d) Reputation. To be qualified for jury service a person must not only have a good moral character, he must have a good reputation. If his reputation for morality is bad, he is disqualified even though it can be shown that he is not immoral. Proof of bad reputation is the usual method of proving bad character. Statutes dealing with reputation provide that jurors must be "respectable," "reputable," "of good reputation."

(e) Religious beliefs. Although jurors are persons sworn, statutes at an early period provided that persons having religious scruples against taking an oath might affirm. It may be assumed that these provisions will take care of the person who has no scruples against an oath, but does not have the religious faith necessary to take an oath.

Persons having religious scruples against serving as jurors

are, according to the statutes of at least one state, exempt from jury service. It would seem, however, that persons holding such a belief are so lacking in public-mindedness that they should be declared disqualified for, not merely exempt from, jury service.

A religious belief or practice may be deemed evidence of bad moral character, such as a belief in, or the practice of, polygamy.

Where a person is opposed to the enforcement of a certain law because of his religious beliefs, he is disqualified for jury service in cases involving that law, not because of his religious beliefs, but because of his opposition to the law.

Religious beliefs may be evidence of disqualification for jury service but are not, in themselves, either qualifications or disqualifications for such service.

(f) Political status. Assuming that a person is physically fit for jury service, has average adult intelligence, and is of good moral character, is it necessary that he also be a "citizen" qualified to vote? At an earlier period it was thought desirable to have aliens on juries in certain cases. Residence, not citizenship, was emphasized at common law. With the development of statutory schemes of jury selection it was found convenient to prescribe for jurors whatever qualifications had been prescribed for voters. When it became settled that voters must be citizens, jurors also had to be citizens.

Wherever it is provided that qualifications for jury service are the same as prescribed for voters, a change may be made in the qualifications of voters without much thought being given to its effect on jury service. Women became qualified for jury service in some states by having conferred upon them the right to vote.

As a matter of principle, it seems reasonable to hold that the burdens of jury duty should fall only on persons who have certain political privileges, principally the right to vote.

This approach, however, will lead to an exemption (not a disqualification) of noncitizens and nonvoters from jury service.

Noncitizens or nonvoters are, in practically all instances, persons who have not been in the community long enough to become citizens or voters, or are persons who have not taken a sufficient interest in political privileges to take the steps necessary to acquire them. If they are not settled residents of the community they may or may not have a sufficient interest in the welfare of the community to serve as jurors. If they have lived in the community long enough to acquire citizenship and the right to vote, but have not done so, their failure may properly be taken as evidence of insufficient public-mindedness.

(g) Residence. There are, or have been, at least four unrelated reasons for requiring that a juror reside within a specified area: (1) To obtain jurors who have knowledge of events, values, and persons involved in a particular case. (2) Procedural convenience. (3) To limit the burdens of jury service. (4) To obtain jurors who have an established sense of responsibility for the welfare of the community in which they serve.

(1) At common law jurors were selected from the place in which the particular cause of action arose so they might have a knowledge of the events, values, and persons involved in the case. Residence in the given locality was not a requirement for jury service in general, but for service in the particular case. In relaxing this early requirement statutes gradually expanded the area until it became the county in which the venue was laid, which, finally, came to be the county in which the inquest or trial was held.

(2) With respect to jury service in general, the chief reasons for requiring a certain residence are related to the selection procedure. Selecting officers act, ordinarily, on their own knowledge, which is limited to persons who reside

nearby. Summoning officers do not, ordinarily, act outside of their bailiwicks.

(3) The jury service of a particular area should be performed by the residents of that area. Furthermore, jurors should not be required to travel far from their homes for jury service.

(4) Settled residence in a community should, and ordinarily does, give a person some sense of responsibility for the welfare of the community. In performing a public service for the community a resident is conscious of the condemnation which will follow if the service is not well performed. It must be recognized, however, that many settled residents are not public-minded. A proper attitude toward the community cannot be assumed from mere residence.

While it may be proper to exempt nonresidents from jury service, and to provide, as a matter of procedural convenience, that only residents be summoned, it seems improper to classify nonresidents as disqualified.

(h) Economic status. If a person is physically fit for jury service, has average adult intelligence, is of good moral character, is a voter, and is a settled resident of the community, should he also be a property-owner in order to be qualified for jury service? Assuming, but not conceding, that the average property owner has a greater sense of responsibility for the welfare of the community than has the average person who does not own property, it must be recognized that a particular juror is not an average person, but is an individual who must be judged on his own merits. While it is clear that a sense of responsibility for a proper administration of justice in the community is, or should be, a requirement for jury service, it is not clear that this subtle qualification can be determined by mechanical tests such as residence, economic status, or social position.

(i) Social position. What has been said with respect to economic status applies equally to social position. While it

may be true that persons of high social position in the community are, as a class, more concerned with public welfare than are persons of low social position, no conclusion from this general fact, if it is a fact, can be drawn with respect to any particular person.

English statutes provide that special juries should be made up of persons legally entitled to be called "esquires," persons of "higher degrees," "bankers or merchants," etc. Early American statutes excluded from jury service "unfree" persons and persons whose color placed them in a low social position. Attempts are still made in some localities to exclude from jury service persons whose low social position is due to color. The latter practice being unconstitutional, the chief remaining trace of social position as a qualification for jury service is to be found in the statutes which limit jury service to the property-owning class.

(j) No criminal record. Having been convicted of certain crimes is a special disqualification for jury service according to the statutes of many states. Conviction of crime may be considered evidence of a bad moral character. Reputation, also, is involved. Some early statutes indicate that the disqualification was based, originally, on the idea that a person guilty of certain crimes is not qualified to take an oath.

(k) No prior jury service. Having served as a juror within a certain time is, from one viewpoint, a temporary disqualification; from another viewpoint, a temporary exemption. If the object of the statute is to curb the use of "professional" jurors, it is a disqualification. If the object is to distribute the burdens of jury duty, it is an exemption.

(l) Not a volunteer. Having volunteered for jury service is made a disqualification in some jurisdictions in an attempt to eliminate the "professional" juror.

(m) Not exempt. Some statutes provide that exempt persons shall not be listed or summoned for jury service. By doing so they turn all exemptions into disqualifications.

If a selecting officer should, without statutory authority, adopt a practice of not listing or summoning exempt persons, he would in effect create disqualifications not provided by statute. Any practice of systematically refusing to list or summon a certain class of persons has this undesirable effect.

2. Service in a Particular Inquest or Trial

(a) Special knowledge. It is possible to select as jurors for a particular inquest or trial persons having two types of special knowledge: (1) Knowledge of the events, values, and persons involved in the cause, including a knowledge of the trustworthiness of the witnesses who will testify in the cause. (2) Knowledge of methods, practices, and customs involved in the cause, such as the methods of carrying on certain businesses.

(1) At early common law jurors were expected to decide cases from their own knowledge. This being true, the jurors, or some of them, had to be summoned from the place where the case arose. A trace of this practice will be found in constitutions and statutes which require a jury of the vicinage for certain inquests and trials. Such a provision for criminal cases is now looked upon as fixing the place of trial; not as requiring jurors who have a personal knowledge of the persons and matters involved in the trial. But even so, there is an occasional reference to the fact that jurors of the vicinage may be able to decide the facts better than other jurors because of their knowledge of the personal qualities of the parties and their witnesses. Where a jury of the vicinage is required for an inquest to condemn land, a principal reason for the requirement is the assumption that persons residing near the land have knowledge of land values in the vicinity not possessed by persons who do not reside near the land.

(2) Early statutes authorized special juries for causes which were of "too great nicety" or "intricacy" for "or-

dinary" jurors. The original idea was to provide "expert" jurors for difficult cases. Although a special jury was ordered for a particular case, the special qualifications were not, in reality, qualifications for the particular case, but for the class of cases to which the particular case belonged. For cases involving the custom of merchants, juries of merchants could be summoned and sworn. For inquests to determine pregnancy, juries of women might be called. It should be noted, also, that qualifications for special juries were not limited to special knowledge of matters which untrained persons might not readily understand. Other special qualifications such as ownership of more property than owned by ordinary jurors, and higher social positions, might also be required. Upon the development of elaborate jury lists, and the discarding of social and property qualifications for jury service, the scheme of providing "expert" jurors for difficult cases largely disappeared.

(b) Impartiality. Constitutions and statutes commonly provide that jurors shall be "impartial." It is at once apparent that this requirement is not a qualification for jury service in general, but is a qualification which a juror must have for service in a particular inquest or trial. In determining whether a proposed juror is "impartial," answers to four questions may have to be considered: (1) Is he opposed to the law involved in the particular case? (2) Does he have an opinion concerning the facts of the case? (3) Is he biased for or against any of the parties to the case? (4) Is he interested (financially) in the outcome of the case? Some statutes deal with the various phases of partiality under the head of "bias." Actual bias is a present state of mind proved as a fact. Implied bias is a presumed state of mind. Many statutes provide, implicitly if not expressly, that certain states of mind shall be presumed (conclusively) from certain facts. The four kinds of bias indicated by the above questions will be discussed separately:

(1) If a person is so opposed to a statute or other law which

may have to be enforced in a particular case that he is unwilling to enforce it, he is disqualified to serve as a juror in that case. This is a matter of actual bias, there being ordinarily no statutory presumptions of this type of bias. Statutes specifically provide that persons opposed to the death penalty may not serve as jurors in the trial of offenses punishable by death. A federal statute provides that persons who believe in polygamy may be excluded from juries impaneled in prosecutions for polygamy.

(2) If a person holds an opinion as to the truth of "facts" which must be proved in the particular case, and is not able to put his opinion aside so as to be guided solely by evidence produced in court, he is disqualified to serve as a juror because of actual bias. Courts have held that disqualifying bias of this type may be presumed from the mere fact that the person has held or expressed an opinion on the facts, but this view has been discarded. Some statutes provide that a person may not serve as a juror if he was a member of the grand jury which found the indictment involved in the particular case; if he has served as arbitrator in the same controversy; if he has served as a juror on a previous trial of the same cause. Persons subpoenaed as witnesses in a particular case may not serve as jurors in that case. These specific statutory disqualifications are based, at least in part, on the presumption that the persons mentioned have formed opinions as to the facts which they cannot lay aside.

(3) Statutes commonly provide that bias for or against a party to a suit must be presumed from certain facts. A person who is the party's "master," "servant," "counsellor," "steward," "attorney," or who is "of kin" to the party is disqualified to serve as a juror in the particular case. The obvious basis of the disqualification is presumed bias *for* the party. If a person is disqualified because he has "an action pending between him and the party," the basis is bias *against* the party. The relationship between the party and the prospective juror may be so remote that a statute

will declare that the relationship shall not disqualify. A statute of this type provides that certain employees of the United States shall be qualified to serve as jurors in prosecutions conducted in the name of the United States.

(4) If a person has a financial interest in the outcome of a particular inquest or trial, he is, usually, presumed to be biased. Where the interest is slight, such as the interest all taxpayers in a city have in the outcome of an action against the city, a statute may declare that the interest is not sufficient to disqualify. An owner of property in a township is sometimes declared disqualified to sit as a juror in an inquest to condemn other property in the township. In the one case a presumption of bias is not to be drawn; in the other, the presumption must be drawn although the juror's interest, if any, is slight.

B. Persons Exempt from Jury Service

1. Public officers and employees

For purposes of jury selection public officers and employees may be classified in three ways: (1) Those whose functions are policy-forming and those whose functions are not policy-forming. (2) Those who are paid for their services and those who are not paid for their services. (3) Those who devote substantially all of their time to the office or employment and those who do not. If their functions are policy-forming they must perform them in person; if not policy-forming, performance by substitutes will do as well. If the public servant is paid for his services he has no basis for seeking relief from the burdens of jury service. If his public services are voluntary, it may be found desirable to exempt him from jury service in order to equalize the burdens of public service. If the officer or employee is not active in his office or employment there is no reason for exempting him from jury service.

Statutes which exempt specified officers and employees usually list (a) officers whose functions are policy-forming and (b) employees for whom substitutes are not readily available. Early statutes expressly recognized the principle of exempting from jury service persons who were performing, or had performed, on a volunteer basis certain other public services. Sometimes the exemption from jury service was granted for life. Some statutes "excuse" only those officers who are actually performing the duties of their offices.

2. Persons engaged in certain professions.

In considering whether persons engaged in certain professions should be exempt from jury service, three questions should be asked: (1) Are the services of the profession so personal in nature that, ordinarily, they must be performed by a certain member of the profession, and not by another? (2) Must the services be rendered at times which cannot be postponed? (3) Is the person involved actively engaged in the practice of his profession? The professions usually listed in exemption statutes are those concerned with health, spiritual affairs, education, and legal counsel. Most services rendered in these professions meet the tests suggested above. Some statutes limit the exemption to persons who are active in the practice of the profession. Many statutes, however, fail to include this important limitation.

3. Persons engaged in certain businesses.

Statutes which exempt persons engaged in certain types of work in certain businesses commonly recognize a distinction between businesses which are strictly private, and those affected with a public interest. They do not, however, adequately recognize that substituted service in a business, though inconvenient and expensive from the viewpoint of business, is not undesirable from the viewpoint of the public. Exemption statutes, passed in periods of labor scarcity, may not suit periods in which the supply of labor is abundant. In principle, exemptions should be granted only where they serve a public, as distinguished from a private, interest.

4. Women.

Women who have the responsibilities of maintaining

homes and rearing children render services which are personal in nature and which cannot, ordinarily, be properly performed by substitutes. If their services are not performed at the times required, the public interest may suffer. There is, on the other hand, no reason why women not having such duties should be exempt from jury service.

5. Persons over a certain age.

If it is presumed that a person over a certain age (60, 65, or 70) is physically or mentally unfit for jury service, being over the maximum age is a disqualification. If it is presumed that such a person has carried his share of the burden of jury service, an upper age limit is an exemption intended to equalize the burdens of public service.

6. Persons who have served as jurors within a certain time.

As pointed out above, a statute which excludes a person from jury service for a certain period of time after he has served as a juror sets up a disqualification or an exemption, depending on whether the object of the statute is to limit the use of "professional" jurors, or is to distribute the burdens of jury service.

C. Persons Excused from Jury Service

1. "Excuse" distinguished from "Disqualification" and "Exemption."

A disqualified person may not serve as a juror even though he is willing to do so. An exempt person may serve or not at his election. An excused person is one who is allowed for special reasons to postpone his turn of jury duty.

2. Specific ground of excuse.

Instead of exempting members of certain professions or persons holding certain public offices regardless of whether they are active in such professions and offices, some statutes provide that these persons shall be "excused" if it appears at the time that they are actually engaged in the work of the profession or public office. When the fact appears, excuse is mandatory; not a matter of discretion. Ill health of a prospective juror or of a member of his family is a specific ground of excuse under some statutes. It should be noted, however, that where a person summoned as a juror is too ill to serve, his illness should be considered a temporary disqualification rather than a ground for excuse. Discharge because of temporary disqualification or because of claimed exemption is often miscalled "excuse."

3. General grounds of excuse.

As expressed in an early statute, a person should be excused from jury service whenever "the interests of the public, or of the individual juror, will be materially injured" by his attendance. In applying these standards it is important to remember that an "excuse" is merely a postponement of the person's turn of service. If service at a later time will be just as injurious as service at the present time, an excuse cannot properly be given. Repeated excuses to prevent the same injury cannot be given without in effect granting an exemption not provided by statute. . . .

* * *

COMPOSITION OF JURIES AS A GROUP

Mr. Holbrook, a distinguished researcher, has compiled some interesting and valuable figures on the actual status of jurors in a particular court at a particular time. From it can be seen the difficulty in obtaining the desired cross section of the community.

I. The Problem

In securing juries, there is always the problem of obtaining the services of a true cross-section of the population without calling upon those whose normal work is indispens-

James G. Holbrook, "Role of Juries in Judicial Administration," A Survey of Metropolitan Trial Courts—Los Angeles Area. *Los Angeles: Parker & Sons, Inc., 1956. Copyright 1956 by The University of Southern California. Reprinted with permission of the copyright holder. Footnotes have been omitted.*

able to the community, or who would suffer financial hardship.

Many of the trial attorneys indicated that they did not feel that the jurors serving represented a true cross section. Among the complaints most often heard were that there were too many housewives and retired people and not enough executives or craftsmen. The judges were interviewed on this question and a significant minority, seventeen superior court judges, twelve judges of the Los Angeles Muncipal Court, and seven of the judges of the outlying municipal courts, confirmed the views expressed by the attorneys. The majority of the judges (fifty-four superior court judges, twenty judges of the Los Angeles Municipal Court, and twenty-two of the judges of the outlying municipal courts), indicated that in their opinion there was a reasonable cross-section of the population serving on juries. The judges were asked (regardless of their answer to the question on "reasonable cross section") to indicate which groups were over- and under-represented. Except for scattered comment, their replies are indicated in the following table.

JUDGES' ESTIMATE OF OVER- AND UNDER-REPRESENTED GROUPS

JURIES—LOS ANGELES COUNTY	SUPERIOR	LOS ANGELES MUNICIPAL	OUTLYING MUNICIPAL	TOTAL
Over-represented:				
Women and housewives	33	21	9	63
Retired	12	7	8	27
Employed (including white-collar, labor, self-employed)	5	2	1	8

Under-represented:				
Businessmen	11	6	8	25
Men	10	9	0	19
Employed (including white-collar, labor, defense workers, self-employed)	18	4	7	29
Professional and executive	10	7	5	22

II. Judicial Suggestions

When asked to suggest what remedies might improve the situation and attract a wider group to jury service, the most repeated suggestion was a more intensive campaign to get employers to make up salary loss. Eighty-four judges were in favor of this idea, while only ten rejected it. Inquiry as to other possible remedies yielded the following responses:

POLICY ON EXCUSING JURORS

(As indicated by responses to questionnaires)

	JUDGES IN FAVOR	JUDGES OPPOSED
Should statutory excuses be curtailed?	19	59
Should the juror's term of service be shortened?	19	59
Should jury fees be increased?	43	42
Should a more rigid denial policy on excusing jurors be adopted?	44	40

III. Composition

The following information concerning composition of juries was compiled from answers to 2,177 jurors' questionnaires returned to this survey.

(a) Sex. The cross section of jurors answering the questionnaire of this survey was representative of those jurors actually serving at least with respect to the ratio of men to women. Our returns showed that 65 per cent of the superior court jurors answering the questionnaire were women, while 64 per cent of the persons listed on the master rolls and the master panel lists of the superior court were women. In the municipal court, 62 per cent of the jurors answering the questionnaire were women and the panel lists showed 62 per cent as women.

When one considers that the census figures of 1950 for the city of Los Angeles show that the ratio of men to women twenty-one years of age and over was forty-seven to fifty-three, the nearly two to one ratio of women to men on jury lists appears high. These figures confirm the comment earlier mentioned that women as a group are over-represented on juries.

(b) Age. The age groupings of jurors answering the questionnaire of this survey were as follows:

AGE CLASSIFICATION OF JURORS

(As indicated by responses to survey questionnaires)

AGE CLASSIFICATION	21–39	40–59	60–70
Superior Court	460—29%	759—48%	369—23%
Municipal Court	195—35%	279—50%	779—14%
Totals	655—31%	1038—48%	448—21%

The superior court had a slightly lower percentage of young people and a higher percentage of the older people than did the municipal court, but each had the bulk of its jurors from the middle group.

(c) Marital Status. The marital status of the jurors responding to query was as follows:

Marital Status of Jurors

(As indicated by responses to survey questionnaires)

MARITAL STATUS	MARRIED	UNMARRIED, WIDOWED, AND DIVORCED
Superior Court	1271—79%	332—21%
Municipal Court	418—77%	125—23%
Totals	1689—79%	457—21%

(d) Education. In terms of education, litigants seemed to have fared surprisingly well in the jurors presented to them. That 43 per cent had at least some college education indicates rather careful screening at some stage on this phase of jury qualifications. We make this comment in view of the fact that the United States census figures for the city show slightly more than 20 per cent of the population had this amount of education. The jurors' responses indicate that another 49 per cent of the jurors had some high school training. This correlates closely with the census figures which show that 48 per cent of the total population had some high school education.

Educational Status of Jurors

(As indicated by responses to survey questionnaires)

EDUCATIONAL STATUS	SUPERIOR COURT	MUNICIPAL COURT
College Degree	30%	29%
College Non-Graduate	13%	11%
High School Graduate	46%	50%
High School Non-Graduate	3%	1%
Grammar School Only	8%	8%

(e) Occupation. When one scans the occupational groupings of jurors it is apparent that housewives are dispropor-

tionately represented and thus present a seeming off-balance of one type of perspective and experience. A possible explanation for this might be that housewives can serve without a loss of earnings, and may have more time available than some of the other groups.

If this were the only explanation, one might also expect the percentage of retired and unemployed persons to be disproportionately high, but both these groups constituted a relatively low percentage of jurors serving.

Note that the percentages indicated in the table do not bear out the comments of judges and attorneys that retired persons are over-represented.

OCCUPATIONAL GROUPINGS OF JURORS

(As indicated by responses to survey questionnaires)

OCCUPATIONAL STATUS	SUPERIOR COURT	MUNICIPAL COURT	TOTALS
Housewives	657—43%	198—37%	855—41%
Clerical	199—13%	73—14%	272—13%
Retired	153—10%	26— 5%	179— 9%
Craftsmen	137— 9%	77—15%	214—10%
Executives	128— 8%	26— 5%	154— 7%
Professional	111— 7%	35— 7%	146— 7%
Sales	79— 5%	39— 7%	118— 6%
Service	38— 2%	28— 5%	66— 3%
Miscellaneous	20— 1%	16— 3%	36— 2%
Operators	6—.4%	10— 2%	16—.8%
Unemployed	5—.3%	2—.4%	7—.3%
Agriculture	1—.1%	0— 0%	1—.1%

* * *

XIII

JURY DELIBERATION

REPORT ON THE JURY PROJECT

The jury project undertaken by the University of Chicago Law School is producing an amazing amount of information about the jury. Published reports indicate that much of the intuitive feelings of lawyers about the value of the jury as a decision-making device has been confirmed. The following two reports indicate some of the facts about jury deliberations reported by the University of Chicago Law School researchers.

. . . We have been concerned, in our own thinking about the jury, with the process by which unanimity is reached, in the degree to which the deliberation produces real changes in position, in the differential opportunities for adjustment and compromise that different types of cases afford the jury, and in what the consequences of relaxing the unanimity requirement are likely to be. The study discloses that in some 71% of the cases the jury was not unanimous on the first ballot, and that in some 36% the split was at least 8 to 4. What, then, is the ultimate fate of the minority view? Does it ever prevail? Does it hang the jury? Or does it always slowly yield? In 90% of the cases in which a majority voted guilty on the first ballot, the verdict was guilty; in 97% of the cases in which the majority voted not guilty on the first ballot, the verdict was not guilty. In the few cases in which the jury was evenly split on the first ballot, the final verdicts were guilty in 50% of the instances and not guilty in 50%.

A second preliminary result from the interviews is that the only instances of hung juries were in cases where the initial vote showed a substantial minority. There were no hung juries where the minority originally was one or two. Hung juries, as you perhaps know, are relatively infrequent. It has been surmised that they result chiefly from the personality of the "hanging juror" and would be eliminated by relaxing the unanimity rule. The figures suggest the competing hypothesis that the hung jury is a function of the closeness of the case itself and perhaps of the moral support that a man feels when his minority view has at least several other supporters.

* * *

A third segment of this study is concerned with attitudes toward jury service. Briefly, the results show that of the jurors who actually sat on a case and did not suffer an economic loss, some 80% would like to serve again; whereas if they did not get to serve on a case and did lose money as a result of service, only some 48% would like to serve again. Further, if they lost money but did sit, the percentage rose to 62%. If the jurors did not sit but did not lose money the percentage was 73%. When asked what suggestions they had for improving the system, 32% of those making suggestions favored elimination of waste of time and 21% favored more pay for jurors. These figures then indicate generally an affirmative response to jury service but point up the two well-known burdens of such service: the waste of the time of the juror who is called but rejected repeatedly on *voir dire,* and the economic loss that jury service may entail for some citizens.

We have several other lines of information on the general question of attitudes toward jury service. One source has been an intensive public opinion survey of attitudes toward the court, jury, and administration of justice generally in a city of moderate size. A sample of those who had jury service in the last year and a sample of the general population were interviewed. The results of this survey are now being analyzed.

The survey discloses, for example, that some 6% of the general population had had jury service at some time during their life and that for 3% this was their only direct contact with the court system. However, some 50% had been in court in some capacity, including 23% who had been a party to litigation and 21% who had been witnesses. Again, some 55% of the general public had known someone who had been a juror. Although it is estimated that some 1,000,000 Americans serve on juries each year, it would appear that jury service is no longer, if it ever was, the dominant avenue for direct citizen contact with the court system, but does remain an important source of indirect contact.

The study contains some striking data on the impact of jury service. Among those who had never served, only 36% said they would like to serve, 16% were undecided, and some 48% said they would not like to serve. However, among those who had served within the last year 94% said they would like to serve again, 3% were willing to serve again as a duty, and only 3% said they would dislike it. These figures cannot be read as indicating that 46% changed their view of jury service after serving. Because of the opportunities for avoiding service, those who do serve in effect choose to do so and are very probably more favorable to the jury at the outset. Making this adjustment, it does appear, however, that some 15% did shift from an unfavorable to a favorable view as a result of serving. Some basis for a reversal of attitude seems to be found in the reasons usually given for disliking jury service in advance. These reasons go largely to the person's uneasiness about judging others, about undergoing a strange new experience, and to his diffidence about his competence. These are reasons which might understandably be dispelled by the actual experience and by its compensating opportunities for excitement and participation in something serious and important. They corroborate our over-all impression that most jurors are exceedingly serious about their job. A tentative conclusion, therefore, is that although in many communities people notoriously seek to avoid jury service, once they are required to submit to it they find it a rewarding and significant experience.

The study also probed along a second line. Respondents were asked, "Which do you think is the better way to have a case decided?" Among the general public some 70% favored the jury, 21% were undecided, and 9% favored trial by judge alone. Among those who had had jury service within the past year 77% favored jury trial, while those favoring bench trial rose to 15%. We have also a comparable set of figures as part of a juror questionnaire given to federal jurors in the Tenth Circuit on which our staff collaborated with a special committee of the bar. Here prior to service some 65% favored jury trial, and after service the figure dropped to 58%; conversely, prior to service 23% favored bench trials, and after service the percentage rose to 33%. However, while 19% of those originally favoring a jury shifted to a judge trial after service, some 17% of those originally favoring a bench trial shifted, after service, to a preference for jury trial.

The respondents showed some tendency to discriminate the type of case in which they preferred a jury. Thus when asked specifically, only 5% of the sample of the general public preferred a judge in criminal cases as against 28% in contract cases. And for those with recent jury service 10% preferred a judge in criminal cases as against 55% in contract cases. These refinements suggest that the general question about preference for judge or jury trial may frequently be understood by the respondent as a question about criminal trials, and further that jury experience perhaps tends to keep one enthusiastic about the jury in a criminal case and make him less enthusiastic about it in the contract case.

Finally, we have some evidence coming from our use of experimental juries, to which I will turn in detail in a few moments. The jurors who were given an experimental negligence case to decide were asked whether they would prefer judge or jury trials in a negligence case if they were the plaintiff and if they were the defendant. Those who would prefer trial by judge in both situations gave mean awards in the experimental case of $14,000. Those who would prefer trial by jury in both situations gave mean awards of $38,000. The data thus suggest strongly the interesting conclusion that preference for trial by jury in negligence cases may tell us something about the person as well as about the jury.

* * *

I shall attempt here only a few illustrations out of the data from the first experimental moot case. The case involves an auto accident in which the plaintiff, a 40-year-old stenographer, was injured when the car in which she was riding as a passenger collided at an intersection with the auto driven by the defendant. The facts were strongly suggestive that the defendant had been negligent in going through a stop sign at high speed. The testimony shows further that the plaintiff suffered a fractured leg and other injuries and had accrued medical expenses and loss of wages at the time of trial. The chief point of controversy, however, was the degree to which she was permanently disabled, and on this there was sharply conflicting medical testimony.

The experimental design of the moot case permitted us to test the effect of several variables at the same time. In three treatments, liability was very clear; in three it was made somewhat ambiguous by modifying the details about the defendant going through the stop sign. These two versions were then combined with three different treatments of defendant's insurance. In the first, defendant on cross-examination reveals he has no insurance, but there is no objection or further attention paid to the disclosure; in the second, the defendant reveals on cross-examination that he has liability insurance, the defendant's counsel objects, and the court directs the jury to disregard this testimony; in the third treatment, the defendant again discloses insurance on cross-examination, but there is no objection and further notice is taken. By combining these two variations of liability and these three variations of insurance disclosure, we get *six* different versions of the basic case which differ however only in these respects and are otherwise identical. The tapes were then played to sets of juries operating under the unanimity rule and to sets of juries operating under a ¾ majority rule. In all, the experiment was given to 30 moot juries, giving us 30 verdicts to score and 360 individual juror pre-deliberation and post-deliberation awards as well.

I should like to indicate very briefly some of the results of this moot case. First, 28 verdicts were in favor of the plaintiff, one jury hung on the damage issue, and one jury found for the defendant. Second, the mean award of all verdicts where liability was clear was $41,000; the mean award of all verdicts where liability was somewhat ambiguous was $34,000. This supports the conclusion that the jury tends to combine the liability and damage issues and confirms a long-held suspicion of the bar that the amount of damages awarded is a variable of the clarity of proof of liability as well as of the clarity of proof of damages. The process is a complex one affecting both the compromise adjustments in the deliberation and the individual juror's own judgment about the quantum of damages. Thus the mean pre-deliberation awards of the individual jurors reflect an almost identical reduction of damages in the treatments where liability has been made ambiguous. Third, no significant difference in award level resulted between juries operating under the unanimity rule and juries operating under the ¾ majority rule.

Fourth, there are the results of the three insurance treatments. Where the defendant disclosed he had no insurance the mean award of all verdicts was $33,000; where he disclosed he had insurance but no further notice was paid to it by court or counsel the mean award rose to $37,000; and where the defendant had insurance and the jury was explicitly told by the court to disregard it, the mean award rose to $46,000. Further, these regularities were equally prominent under each of the liability versions of the case scored separately. The subtlety of the jurors' response to insurance is indicated by two other lines of data. The post-deliberation awards of the 360 individual jurors once again showed the highest award where the court had explicitly instructed the jury to disregard insurance. Finally, the deliberations were inspected and scored for the frequency of mentions of insurance under the three treatments. In the 10 deliberations in which insurance was disclosed but no notice taken of it there were a total of 61 insurance mentions, 46% of which carried an implication for raising damages; in the 10 deliberations where the court explicitly ordered insurance to be disregarded there were only 36 mentions of insurance, 19% of which carried an implication for increasing damages. We are tempted to conclude therefore that instructing the jury about insurance will tend to keep them talking about it, but will also tend to increase the frequency with which they do something affirmative about it.

The insurance data throw some light on a familiar policy dilemma in the administration of tort law through the jury. There are a series of points on which the law is clear, such as insurance, counsel fees, nontaxability of personal injury damages, etc., but on which it is most difficult to say whether it would be better policy explicitly to instruct the jury to disregard or, as is generally the practice today, to be silent on the point. Our experimental jury data do suggest that the instruction on the forbidden practice tends to aggravate the consequence the instruction is intended to prevent. We have not as yet experimented directly with instructions on awarding counsel fees as part of plaintiff's damages, but the post-trial interviews with the experimental jurors indicate that some 38% did consider such fees and as a result raised their awards. And this is, of course, a frequent point of explicit discussion in the moot deliberations themselves, it often appearing that the jurors sense no impropriety in awarding such fees. The data on the tax point in the experimental juries are slender but indicate that some 5% of the jurors raised the award on the double misconception that it was income taxable and that they were permitted to increase damages accordingly.

One further point of general interest to tort law is suggested by this first experimental routine. It will be recalled that the plaintiff was a passenger in one of the colliding autos. There was some possibility from the testimony of concluding that her driver was also negligent. The jury was given a standard instruction against imputing the negligence of the driver to the plaintiff. But the deliberations on occasion suggest that imputing negligence is a more popular sentiment than the law recognizes, and some 23% of the jurors in post-trial interview indicated they had considered the point and had lowered the damages as a result. It appears too from inspection of the moot deliberations that the jury may reach its result not by charging the negligence of the driver to the passenger directly but rather by saying that since both drivers are negligent the damages should not all be assessed against the one who happens to have been sued. These preliminary data are thus suggestive of the difficulties in application of certain basic tort concepts. The jury may impute negligence of a third party to the plaintiff but then use a comparative negligence approach to modify the damage awards, thus deviating in two respects from the law, but following a logic that has much to commend it.

You will recall the data on the high frequency with which first ballot votes in the jury interview study coincide with the final verdict. The experimental data, at least where damages are highly controversial, indicate a quite different pattern. It is true that the mean value of all 30 verdicts and all 360 pre-deliberation awards is the same, namely $38,000. This does not mean, however, that the verdicts in individual experimental cases are simply quotient verdicts, that is, the average of the twelve pre-deliberation awards. Inspection of the pre-deliberation awards on a case-by-case basis indicates that there may be very considerable adjustment of view in the deliberation, so that the final verdict may differ substantially from the mean pre-deliberation award of those twelve jurors. It indicates too how difficult the jury's task of reaching consensus may be, given the initial wide divergence of views ranging from no liability at all up through awards of $100,000.

A closely related point involves the comparison of the pre- and post-deliberation awards. The similarity of the post-deliberation awards to the verdicts is a measure of the growth of consensus during the deliberation, and conversely the difference can be taken as a measure of the degree of compromise effected during the deliberation. Further comparison of the pre-deliberation award to the post-deliberation award can be taken as a measure of the degree of persuasion achieved by the deliberation discussion. I shall not pause for the details of such comparisons here, but the point is that the experimental routine appears to offer an excellent framework in which to work toward a general theory of the impact of the group deliberation on the individual juror's judgment.

We have, as I said, marked up three experimental cases. A second involves the defense of insanity in a prosecution for housebreaking. Here we seek to test the difference in jury response to the traditional M'Naghten definition of legal insanity in criminal cases and the new mental defect test put forward by Judge Bazelon in the recent *Durham* case.

A third case involves questions of manufacturer and retailer liability where a vaporizer allegedly causes a fire severely burning the infant plaintiff. Here damages are clearly substantial, but liability is highly ambiguous and both negligence and warranty theories of liability are in the case. The principal variable sought to be tested here is the effect of interrogatories for a special verdict. In one set of runs the jury operates under conventional general verdict procedure; in a second set of runs the jury operates under special verdict procedure and is given 16 interrogatories; in a third set of runs the jury, again under a general verdict, is given no substantive instructions of law other than the instruction to do justice and equity. The first 18 runs of this experiment have now been completed and are being analyzed. I might, however, note an interesting development from the first deliberation. There is some evidence in the case on the point of whether the child's mother left the vaporizer on too long or used it in a dangerous way. The interrogatories deal with this question in two ways. They ask whether the mother was using the vaporizer in accordance with the printed instructions. They also ask whether the mother failed to exercise that degree of care which an ordinarily prudent person would have exercised under like circumstances, and if so, was this lack of care such that it became the intervening cause. In this first experimental run the jury, after considerable difficulty, answered yes to the following of printed instructions and no to the question of whether the mother's lack of care was the sole intervening cause. But in assessing the damages the jury apportioned the negligence in equal thirds among the mother, the manufacturer, and the drug company, and therefore reduced the damages by two thirds. The example indicates once again the powerful pull on the jury of the notion of apportioning fault among all those responsible for the damage, including the plaintiff. But most interesting, it indicates the jury was able to do this despite the interrogatories and without giving inconsistent answers to them.

Judges v. Juries

It has been repeatedly indicated in the discussion that a central question about the jury is the degree to which judges would decide cases differently from juries. And this is an appropriate point with which to conclude. We have had three converging lines of inquiry on the areas of judge-jury comparisons. The individual case studies through juror interviews included, you may recall, interviews with the judge. We thus have for these cases the view the judge had of the case. A second line of inquiry has utilized the experimental jury routine. The experimental auto negligence case was given to a group of trial and appellate judges for decision. Several of the results are of interest. The mean award of the judges was $32,500 as compared with the experimental jury average verdict of $34,000 for the same version of the case—a striking similarity. You will recall that the juries gave their highest award in the variation where the court had explicitly instructed them to ignore the disclosure of insurance. The judges, however, gave their lowest award in this instance. However, the judges' awards did vary with the presence or absence of insurance; the award going from $32,500 where the defendant was revealed to have no insurance to $40,300 where the defendant disclosed he had insurance but no further notice was taken of it.

There is one further point in this data of possibly wide significance. There was considerable variation in the verdicts of the experimental juries, but the variation was markedly less than that of the individual juror pre-deliberation awards. The data thus tend to confirm the hypothesis that one consequence of having juries decide as a group of twelve is to cut significantly the variation in individual juror decision. The group thus acts as an important control device for moderating the possible eccentricity of individual juror judgment. Further, the awards of the individual judges vary approximately as much as those of the individual juries. There is thus some preliminary support for the engaging hypothesis that it takes a group of twelve jurors to produce as small a variance as the single judge. Or to put this less technically, twelve jurors will tend to decide cases much more like the judge than would single jurors. I should add parenthetically that the experimental design has furnished a useful mode for analysis of certain problems of jury administration by permitting us to repeat trials of the same case. One test of certain legal rules therefore may be their tendency to reduce the variation in jury verdicts in the same case and in that sense to increase the stability of jury decision-making.

The major line of comparison of judge and jury decision-making has been the questionnaire on which some 500 state and federal trial judges throughout the United States have cooperated. The judge is asked to enter on the questionnaire the decision he would have made in the case had there been no jury trial, and to give certain additional information about the issues in the case, the procedures used, and his explanation when there is a divergence between his decision and that of the jury. It is understood that the information will be used for statistical purposes only. At present some 5,000 questionnaires have been returned by judges covering some 3,000 civil and some 2,000 criminal cases decided during the past year. The data are currently being analyzed and admit of considerable refinement, but some preliminary results are now available for 1,428 personal injury cases.

In 41% of these cases the judge and jury agreed fully; in 23% the judge would have awarded somewhat less than the jury; and in 17% the judge would have awarded somewhat more than the jury; finally, in 10% of the cases the judge would have found for the defendant where the jury found for the plaintiff, while in 8% of the cases the judge would have found for the plaintiff where the jury found for the defendant. Thus in all, the judge favored the defendant more than the jury in 33% of the cases, which is perhaps close to our expectation. But the quite striking and unexpected result is that the judge would have favored the plaintiff more than the jury in some 25% of the cases. The very widely held view that juries in personal injury cases are more plaintiff prone than judges is thus shown to be a considerable oversimplification.

The various refinements of this data appear to be of interest. I shall give only a few illustrations. Thus if we consider separately cases where the jury found for the defendant, we find the judge in agreement 82% of the time, whereas in cases where the jury found for the plaintiff the judge is in complete agreement only 18% of the time. However, in some 69% of such cases the judge differed from the jury only in the amount of damages and not on liability. Further, in cases where the jury found for the plaintiff, the judge would have given a higher award in 33% of the instances. Again in 13% of the cases where the jury found for the plaintiff the judge would have found no liability, but in 18% of the cases where the jury found for the defendant the judge would have found liability.

The data have been correlated with the length of the jury deliberation and show that the percentage of judge-jury agreement is highest when the deliberation is shortest and declines markedly as the deliberation increases. A similar correlation, although not so marked, appears for the length of the trial.

Again, the data were run for state and federal judges separately and show no significant change in the incidence of agreement and divergence.

One final illustration will have to suffice. The percentage of agreement remains almost constant, whether or not written instructions are given the jury; whether or not the judge summarizes the evidence; and whether or not the judge comments on credibility or on the weight of the evidence. These have been highly controversial issues in recent years, but the data are strongly suggestive of the conclusion that at least in personal injury cases these procedural controls make the jury neither more nor less like the judge.

* * *

XIV

JURY VERDICTS

VERDICTS, GENERAL AND SPECIAL

Professor Sunderland makes a persuasive argument for the special verdict by pointing out that with the special verdict the jury is doing that which it is most capable of doing—"fact finding"—and is not involved in applying the law, a task for which he says it is ill equipped.

The peculiarity of the general verdict is the merger into a single indivisible *residuum* of all matters, however numerous, whether of law or fact. It is a compound made by the jury which is incapable of being broken up into its constituent parts. No judicial reagents exist for either a qualitative or a quantitative analysis. The law supplies the means for determining neither what facts were found, nor what principles of law were applied, nor how the application was made. There are therefore three unknown elements which enter into the general verdict: (*a*) the facts; (*b*) the law; (*c*) the application of the law to the facts. And it is clear that the verdict is liable to three sources of error, corresponding to these three elements. It is also clear that if error does occur in any of these matters it cannot be discovered, for the constituents of the compound cannot be ascertained.

Edson R. Sunderland, "Verdicts, General and Special," 29 Yale Law Journal *253 (1920). Copyright 1920 by Yale Law Journal. Reprinted with permission of the copyright owner.*

No one but the jurors can tell what was put into it and the jurors will not be heard to say. The general verdict is as inscrutable and essentially mysterious as the judgment which issued from the ancient oracle of Delphi. Both stand on the same foundation—a presumption of wisdom. The court protects the jury from all investigations and inquiry as fully as the temple authorities protected the priestess who spoke to the suppliant votary at the shrine. It is quite probable that the law is wise in not permitting jurors to testify as to how they compounded their verdict, for all stability would disappear if such inquiries were open. But it does not follow that there is not some better way of deciding controversies than by means of this mysterious agency. If the compound cannot be subjected to analysis perhaps it can be dispensed with.

As to the first element in the general verdict, the finding of *facts,* it is much better done by means of the special verdict. Every advantage which the jury is popularly supposed to have over the court as a trier of facts, is retained, with the very great additional advantage that the analysis and separation of the facts in the case which the court and the attorneys must necessarily effect in employing the special verdict, materially reduces the chance of error. It is easy to make mistakes in dealing at large with aggregates of facts. The special verdict compels detailed consideration. But above all it enables the public, the parties and the court to see what the jury really has done. The general verdict is either all wrong or all right, because it is an inseparable and inscrutable unit. A single error completely destroys it. But the special verdict enables errors to be localized so that the sound portions of the verdict may be saved and only the unsound portions be subject to redetermination through a new trial. The morale of the jury also is aided by throwing off the cloak of secrecy, for only through publicity is there developed the proper feeling of responsibility in public servants. So far, then, as the facts go, they can be much more effectively, conveniently, and usefully tried by abandoning the general verdict and substituting the special verdict.

As to the second element in the general verdict, the *law,* it is a matter upon which the jury is necessarily ignorant. The jurors are taken from the body of the county, and it is safe to say that the last man who would be called or allowed to sit would be a lawyer. They are second-hand dealers in law, and must get it from the judge. They can supply nothing themselves; they are a mere conduit pipe through which the court supplies the law that goes into the general verdict. But while the jury can contribute nothing of value so far as the law is concerned, it has infinite capacity for mischief, for twelve men can easily misunderstand more law in a minute than the judge can explain in an hour. Indeed, can anything be more fatuous than the expectation that the law which the judge so carefully, learnedly, and laboriously expounds to the laymen in the jury box will become operative in their minds in its true form? One who has never studied a science cannot understand or appreciate its intricacies, and the law is no exception to this rule. The very theory of the jury and its general verdict is thus predicated upon a premise which makes practically certain an imperfect or erroneous view of the principles of law which are to be compounded into the verdict. The instructions upon the law given by the court to the jury are an effort to give, in the space of a few minutes, a legal education to twelve laymen upon the branch of the law involved in the case. Law cannot be taught in any such way. As to this element, accordingly, the general verdict is almost necessarily a failure.

As to the third element in the general verdict—the *application of the law to the facts*—we find the same difficulty as in the case of the first element—a merging of the law into the verdict in such a way that it is impossible to tell how or whether the jury applied the law. They may have applied it in a wholly wrong way, or they may have failed to apply it at all. No analysis of the verdict can be made which will throw any light on the process. Since the case can ordinarily go to the jury only if a verdict either way is legally possible, whatever the jury does is presumed to be right, and this presumption excludes any inquiry from the jurors themselves. Cases may arise where the verdict shows on its face a failure to properly apply the law, usually as relating to the measure of damages, but in the vast majority of cases the verdict is a complete mystery, throwing a mantle of impenetrable darkness over the operations of the jury. Whether the jurors deliberately and openly threw the law into the discard, and rendered a verdict out of their own heads, or whether they applied the law correctly as instructed by the court, or whether they tried to apply it properly but failed for lack of understanding—these are questions respecting which the verdict discloses nothing. So far, therefore, as the third element goes, the general verdict is an unknown and unknowable mystery, with the balance of probability against it.

* * *

We come, then, to this position, that the general verdict is not a necessary feature of litigation in civil actions at law, and that it confers on the jury a vast power to commit error and do mischief by loading it with technical burdens far beyond its ability to perform, by confusing it in aggregating instead of segregating the issues, and by shrouding in secrecy and mystery the actual results of its deliberations. Every one of these defects is absent from the special verdict. Why then should not the general verdict in civil cases be abolished and the special verdict take its place?

* * *

USE OF MAJORITY VERDICTS

STATE	CASES	COURTS	MAJORITY
Alaska	civil	district	5/6
Arkansas	civil	......	9/12
Arizona	civil	superior	any
California	civil	......	3/4
Colorado	civil	......	any
Connecticut	civil	......	9/12
Hawaii	civil	......	any
Idaho	civil	......	3/4
	misdemeanor	......	5/6
Iowa	civil	......	any
Kentucky	civil	circuit	3/4
Louisiana	civil	......	9/12
	crim. less than death penalty	......	9/12
Minnesota	civil	of record	5/6
Mississippi	civil	circuit chancery	3/4
Missouri	civil	not of record	2/3
	civil and below felony	of record	3/4
Montana	civil	......	2/3
Nebraska	civil	......	5/6
Nevada	civil	......	3/4
New Jersey	civil	......	5/6
New Mexico	civil	......	10/12
New York	civil	......	5/6
Ohio	civil	......	3/4
Oklahoma	civil and below felony	......	3/4
Oregon	civil	......	3/4
	crim. other than 1st degree murder	circuit	10/12
Panama Canal	civil	......	3/4
South Dakota	civil	jp & municipal	3/4
		all others	10/12
Texas	civil and below felony	......	9/12 or 9/remaining jurors
Utah	civil	......	3/4
Virginia	civil	......	2/3
Washington	civil	superior	10/12
Wisconsin	civil	......	5/6
Wyoming	civil	......	any
Federal	civil	......	any

"Use of Majority Verdicts in the United States," 33 Journal of the American Judicature Society 111 (December 1949) [with recent additions and changes]. Reprinted with permission of copyright owner.

IN THE UNITED STATES

CONDITIONS	CONST.	STATUTE
......	......	Code. 55-7-81a
......	II-7	Const. amended, 1928
consent	II-23	Code 1939, 21-1001, 21-1003
......	I-7	Deering, C.C.613
consent	......	Rules C.P., 48
consent	I-21	G.S. 1949, 7971 13 Haw. 705
consent	......	(1901)
......	I-7	Code 1947, 2-104
......	I-7	Code 1947, 19-1902
consent	I-9	Code 1946, R.C.P. 203
......	248	Rev. Stat. 1948, 29.330
......	......	CPC 527, 532.10; G.S. 1958
......	VII-41	Crim. Code 338
12 hrs. deliberation	I-4	Stat. Ann. 1945, 546.17
request	III-31	Code, 1942, 1801
......	II-28	Rev. Stat. 1939, 2662
......	II-28	Rev. Stat. 1939, 719
......	III-23	Rev. Code, 1935, 9358
6 hrs. deliberation	I-6	Rev. Stat. 1943, 25-1125
......	I-3	Comp. Laws 1929, 87766
......	......	Rev. Stat. Supp. 1948, 2:27-233.1
......	12	R.C.P., 48
......	1-2	Cahill N.Y.C.P. 1946, 463a
......	I-5	Throckmorton's Code Ann. 1948, 10350
......	II-19	......
......	VII-5	......
......	1-11	......
......	......	C.Z. Code, 4-467
......	VI-6	Code 1939, 33.1334, 33.2808
......	VI-6	Code 1939, 33.1333
signed by jurors	V-13	R.C.P. 292
......	1-10	Code Ann. 1943, 104—24-27
consent	......	Code Ann. 1942, 6012
......	1-21	Rem. Rev. Stat., 1931, 358
......	I-5	Stat. 1947, 270.25
consent	......	R.C.P. 48
consent	......	Fed. R.C.P. 48

XV

DELAY AND THE JURY

DELAY IN COURT

As part of the University of Chicago Jury Project, an attempt was made to pinpoint the cause of delay in court. One aspect of the study sought to answer the question "Do jury trials significantly cause delay in court?" Professors Zeisel, Kalven and Buchholz lay this ghost to rest. After finding that jury trials in New York City take more time than court trials, they discovered that jury trials in New York City also take almost the same amount of additional time as jury trials in New Jersey. The authors say: "The inviting conclusion therefore is that the remedy for delay is not to abolish the jury trial but to speed it up" (as was done in New Jersey).

Speeding up the trial process

To what extent can the trial process itself be speeded up? The most obvious and widely discussed possibility is a shift from jury to bench trial. The difference in length between jury and bench trial on the same case turns out to be a

Hans Zeisel, Harry Kalven, Jr., and Bernard Buchholz, Delay in the Court. *Boston: Little, Brown and Company, 1959.* *Footnotes have been omitted.*

surprisingly difficult point to measure because no case, of course, is ever tried both ways. But a reasonable estimate by various procedures is that a bench trial is on the average about 40 per cent less time-consuming than a jury trial. If the extreme remedy of total abolition of jury trial in personal injury cases were adopted, the saving in the New York Court would be the equivalent of about 1.6 judges per year; and the delay would be removed in 5 to 7 years, depending on whether the abolition of jury trial were made retroactive to pending cases.

These figures can be read in two ways, depending upon one's viewpoint as to the values of jury trial itself. They may impress some with the fact that jury trial is expensive in court time and that the abolition of jury trial offers an effective remedy for delay. Or they may be read, as we ourselves would incline to read them, as a price tag for the jury system. On this view, what is impressive is that the addition of only 1.6 judges per year would net the same impact on delay as the abolition of a basic institution. It may be added, though, that this figure, for reasons which will appear later, is particularly small for the New York Court, and will be relatively larger for most others.

* * *

The possibility of speeding up the jury trial itself has received far less attention than it merits. Several lines of evidence point to a considerable potential here. In New Jersey, roughly comparable cases are tried to a jury in approximately 40 per cent less time than in New York. The savings come not so much from differences in the obvious jury time costs, such as *voir dire* and instructions, as from differences in the internal trial process itself. This may in part result from the efficiency of the New Jersey pre-trial in narrowing issues for trial, although we have no evidence for this. Perhaps the single most surprising finding of the study is that this difference between jury trial in New York and in New Jersey is as large as the much advertised general difference between bench and jury trial. The inviting conclusion therefore is that the remedy for delay is not to abolish the jury trial but to speed it up.

* * *

Estimating the difference in length between a jury trial and a bench trial of the same case turns out to be a good deal more complicated than might be expected. It is easy enough to make a start by comparing the average length of completed jury trials with that of bench trials. Table 1 makes this comparison for a 10-month period for the New York Court.

TABLE 1

AVERAGE LENGTH OF COMPLETED JURY AND BENCH TRIALS OF PERSONAL INJURY CASES IN THE NEW YORK COURT

	JURY TRIAL	BENCH TRIAL
Time (in hours)	17.4	8.9
Number of cases on which average is based	(148)	(75)

This would indicate that a jury trial is longer than a bench trial in a ratio of about 2 to 1, an estimate which has occasionally been used in public discussion. So simple a comparison, however, is unsatisfactory because it involves the assumption that there is no significant difference between the cases which are tried to the judge and the cases which are tried to the jury. There is considerable reason for doubting that this is true. For one thing, waiving the jury trial in a personal injury case is certainly the exception and not the rule in most jurisdictions, even in New York. This suggests that the type of personal injury case which plaintiff counsel is willing to try without a jury is likely to differ on the average from the case he tries before the jury, and that this difference is likely to be reflected in the complexity of the case, and hence in the time required for its disposition.

That these cases are indeed different is corroborated by the comparison shown in Table 2 of jury verdicts and bench judgments in personal injury trials of the Court.

Awards from bench judgments are, on the average, about half the size of the awards made in jury trials. This difference is much too great to be credited to the normal difference between jury and judge looking at the same case. That difference, on the best available evidence, is only about 20 per cent. The remainder of the difference must be due to self-selection: the jury is more likely to be waived in smaller cases. This is also indicated by the smaller number of witnesses in the average bench trial.

It would be clearly a mistake, therefore, simply to accept the average trial time of actual jury and bench trials as a true reflection of the difference which two trials of the same case would produce.

But if the cases that go to the jury are intrinsically dif-

TABLE 2

MAGNITUDE OF JURY AND NON-JURY CASES

AWARD SIZE IN PERSONAL INJURY TRIALS DECIDED FOR THE PLAINTIFF

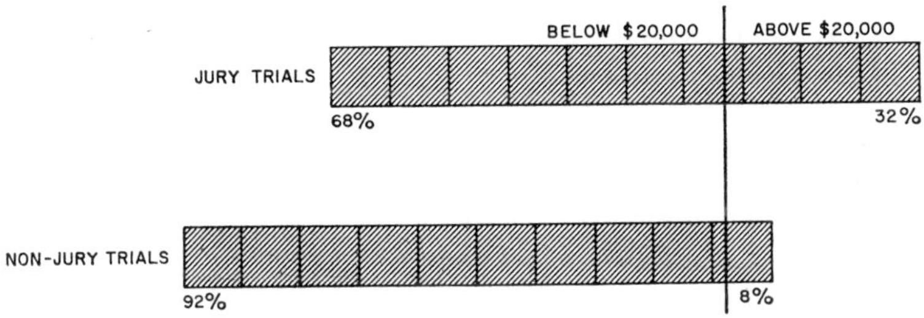

TABLE 3 *

AVERAGE NUMBER OF WITNESSES IN COMPLETED PERSONAL INJURY TRIALS

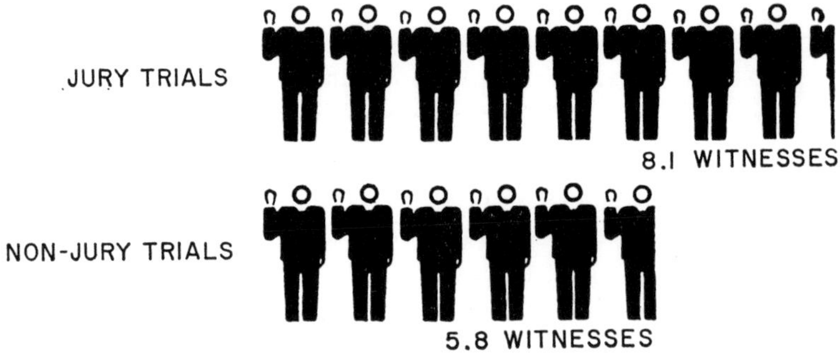

* Court year 1956–1957.

ferent from the cases that go to a bench trial, we are faced with a serious difficulty. What we want to find out is how much less time on the average it would take if a group of cases instead of being tried before a jury were tried before a judge. To be sure, once in a long while it happens that a case tried to a jury is reversed and then tried again with the jury waived. But aside from the rarity of such an event, at the second trial the case is really not the same any more. And since it is quite unthinkable that cases could be tried experimentally twice, it becomes clear that, even with all the time and money for research, it would not be possible to solve the problem with precision. But if we are satisfied with somewhat less than a perfect solution, more substantial insights are possible.

The first research approach we tried served to take us only a short way toward our goal, but it is worth reporting in some detail simply as a further illustration of the difficulty of matching comparable cases. We turned to the federal trial docket. Here we had two types of personal injury suits which ought to be comparable enough, except for their mode of trial. In personal injury cases reaching the federal court because of diversity of citizenship, the plaintiff can demand a jury trial and does so in the great majority of cases. But if such a suit is brought against the United States government, it must be tried, under the Federal Tort Claims Act, to a judge as a matter of law. This offers therefore an opportunity to compare cases tried in jury and bench trials which could not be selectively distributed but had to follow the procedure provided for them by the law. The Administrative Office of the United States Courts recorded for us, for a sample of such comparable cases, the exact time required for their trial. The results are given in Table 4.

On closer analysis, however, it appears that the cases are still not comparable. This is indicated by the fact that the average length of non-jury diversity cases differs from that of the Tort Claims Act non-jury trials, at least in this sample. Samples of 12 and 15 cases are very small, apparently too small, for basing averages on them for trials that vary considerably among themselves. Probably most disturbing for our analysis is the fact that the cases in Table 4 are not all completed trials; some were settled during trial, and the possibility that these trials were terminated at various stages adds another factor of inaccuracy. And for our particular purposes the value of federal court data is somewhat diminished by the fact that, unlike tort cases in the New York Court, they require, as it appears, considerable time in chambers. Thus, we reluctantly conclude that these data yield in the end not much more than another very rough estimate, a ratio of about 2 to 1, for the length of the two modes of trial.

But there remains the possibility of extracting some more useful information from the comparison of actual jury and bench trials in the New York Court, despite the fact that these cases are probably different.

We can try to make jury and bench cases more closely comparable by adjusting for the large difference in the

TABLE 4

LENGTH OF PERSONAL INJURY TRIALS IN THE FEDERAL COURTS

	United States Defendant	*Diversity of Citizenship*	
	NON-JURY	JURY	NON-JURY
Hours spent in			
Chambers	2.3	2.8	2.4
Court	3.9	9.6	5.4
Total	6.2	12.4	7.8
Number of trials in sample	(12)	(64)	(15)

average number of witnesses: 8.1 in jury trials, 5.8 in bench trials. But this adjustment cannot be made by simply assuming an equal number of witnesses for both. There are indications that if the same case were tried before a judge instead of a jury, counsel would on the average put slightly fewer witnesses on the stand. We submitted to a group of leading negligence trial lawyers in New York City a series of questions on the difference between judge and jury trial. A total of 27 questionnaires were returned: 6 from plaintiff attorneys, 11 from defense attorneys, and 10 from attorneys representing both plaintiff or defendant. Since the views of these three groups differed somewhat, their answers were determined separately, and then given equal weight, so as to avoid bias from the accidental fact of having fewer plaintiff counsel in our sample than defense counsel. Among others we asked this question: "As to the number of witnesses: would you say that if the same case were tried *without* a jury, the parties would call more, less, or the same number of witnesses? If more or less: by what percentage?"

The answers were as follows:

COUNSEL FOR	FEWER WITNESSES IN BENCH TRIAL (IN PER CENT)
Plaintiff	0
Plaintiff or defendant	—10
Defendant	—13
Average all three groups	— 8

Essentially the same question was asked of a sample of the trial judges in the New York Court. Five of them replied and their combined estimate was that the number of witnesses in a bench trial of the same case would be 11 per cent smaller. Averaging the two results (8 per cent and 11 per cent) and rounding off, we obtain then 10 per cent as our best estimate of the difference.

The figures from Tables 1 and 3 concerning jury and bench trial, it will be recalled, were as follows:

	JURY TRIAL	BENCH TRIAL
Length (in hours)	17.4	8.9
Number of witnesses	(8.1)	(5.8)

If the "average jury" case were tried as a bench trial it would have (8.1 minus 10% =) 7.3 witnesses. We now apply the "average time per witness" in a bench trial (5.8 into 8.9 =) 1.53 hours to the 7.3 witnesses and obtain (7.5 × 1.53 =) 11.2 hours. This then is the number of hours the 17.4-hour jury trial would have required had it been tried to a judge. The jury trial is 55 per cent longer than the bench trial, or conversely the bench trial 36 per cent shorter than the jury trial.

By a different route we obtained two more estimates of the difference between judge and jury trial. We also had asked our sample of trial judges and lawyers to estimate outright the difference in length between an average personal injury jury trial, and the time it would have taken to try the *same* case without a jury. The combined estimate of the five judges is shown in Table 5.

TABLE 5

JUDGES' ESTIMATE OF DIFFERENCE BETWEEN JURY AND BENCH TRIAL OF AVERAGE PERSONAL INJURY CASE

	AVERAGE LENGTH * (IN HOURS)
Jury trial	16.5
Bench trial	9.1
Difference	7.4 = −45%

* Time for jury impaneling and deliberation excluded.

The trial lawyers estimated the difference as shown in Table 6. Again, we have taken the averages of the three types of lawyers.

TABLE 6

TRIAL LAWYERS' ESTIMATE OF DIFFERENCE BETWEEN JURY AND BENCH TRIAL OF AVERAGE PERSONAL INJURY CASE*

	JURY TRIAL (HOURS)	BENCH TRIAL (HOURS)	DIFFERENCE (PER CENT)
Plaintiff lawyers	11.4	7.9	−31
Defendant lawyers	13.0	6.8	−49
Lawyer for either	13.5	7.8	−40
Average	12.6	7.5	−40

* Time for jury impaneling and deliberation excluded.

We now have three different estimates of the difference between jury and bench trial of the average personal injury case: −36 per cent, −45 per cent, and −40 per cent. Since each of the three estimating procedures has its shortcomings and advantages and since we are sufficiently encouraged by the relative closeness of the results from these quite independent approaches, we shall accept for the purposes of the subsequent analysis, as the best estimate, the average of the

TABLE 7

DIFFERENCE IN LENGTH BETWEEN JURY AND NON-JURY TRIAL

PERSONAL INJURY CASES

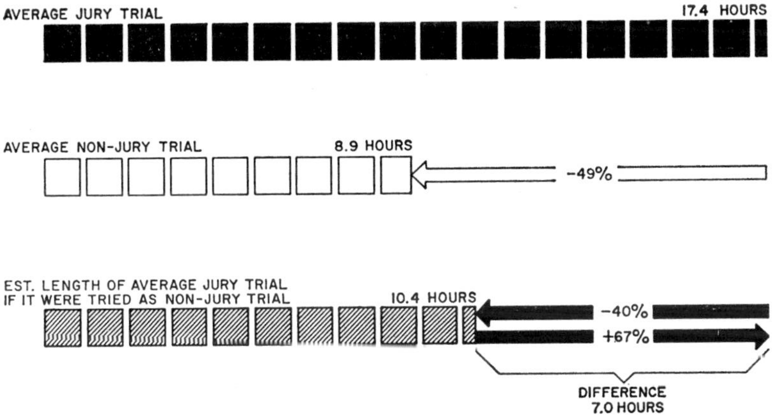

three, that is —40 per cent, as to how much shorter a bench trial is than a jury trial of the same case. Or, looked at the other way around, the jury trial is 67 per cent longer than the bench trial, as shown in Table 7.

It is of interest to see how, in the opinion of our sample of judges, the specific trial elements contribute to the over-all difference, as shown in Table 8.

TABLE 8

JUDGES' DETAILED COMPARISON OF JURY AND BENCH TRIAL

	JURY TRIAL (HOURS)	BENCH TRIAL (HOURS)
Opening statements	0.7	0.3
Taking of evidence	13.9	8.1
Argument on law and closing statements	1.3	0.7
Charge by the court	0.6	
Total	16.5	9.1

(*Voir dire*	2.0)
(Jury deliberation	3.6)

Table 8 makes it apparent that there is a troublesome question as to whether certain items should be included or excluded in counting the length of the trial. For the jury trial there are two such items: the time for *voir dire* and for the jury deliberation; for the bench trial there is the time that may be needed for the judge's deliberation and findings of fact. Clearly, the test is whether these items engage the judge sufficiently from doing anything else. This will vary from jurisdiction to jurisdiction. In New York we decided to exclude all of them. As to *voir dire* in the New York Court, there is little doubt that it should not be included. First because it is usually conducted in the judge's absence, and second because—as a result of the judge's absence—it is usually more time-consuming: to extend the number of permitted peremptory challenges, the institution of "challenge by consent of both counsel" has developed, which takes the place of a very liberally interpreted challenge for cause. The conclusion as to jury deliberation time and judge deliberation time is less clear-cut. We must assume, however, that most of the jury deliberation time will permit the judge to do something else. And while not all bench decisions are rendered immediately at the end of the trial, there is no practice of findings of fact in New York. The safer course, therefore, was to disregard also this item. Insofar as these exclusions introduce inaccuracies to our comparison, they probably offset each other.

One or two other qualifications need to be added. Any over-all estimate of the difference between jury and bench trial implies that both are on the whole conducted by some stable standards of efficiency. But we know that these must vary from court to court, judge to judge, case to case, and especially from lawyer to lawyer. It is even said that the less stringent handling of exclusionary rules in bench cases may sometimes prolong bench trials beyond what a jury trial would require because the judge will admit evidence subject to objection which he would not admit before a jury. And the pressure to avoid continuances in a jury trial must occasionally work for tighter control.

Finally, an exact distinction in our computation between completed trials and cases settled during trial would probably result in a somewhat lower estimate for the time saved through reduction of jury trial. Certainly, part of the difference between jury and bench trial comes at the end of the trial in instructions to the jury, closing arguments and deliberation time. Yet such refinement would tax the relatively crude measure we have so far developed.

With all the indicated limitations, we are satisfied that for New York our figure will serve its purpose, as an estimate of the savings that could be made if any portion of the Court's present jury trials could be converted into bench trials: roughly 40 per cent of the former trial time would be saved.

BIBLIOGRAPHY

Asch, Solomon. *Social Psychology*. Englewood Cliffs, N. J.: Prentice-Hall, Inc., 1952.

Barnlund, D. "A Comparative Study of Individual, Majority, and Group Judgment," *Journal of Abnormal Psychology,* 58 (1959), 55.

Blackstone, Sir William. *Commentaries on the Laws of England,* Vol. III. Adaptation by John L. Wendell. New York: Harper & Brothers, 1854.

Blume, William W. "Jury Selection Analyzed: Proposed Revision of Federal System," 42 *Michigan Law Review* 831 (1944).

Busch, Francis X. "The Jury System in America; Guarantees of Federal and State Constitutions," *Law and Tactics in Jury Trials*. Indianapolis: The Bobbs-Merrill Co., Inc., 1949.

Choate, Joseph H. Annual Address. *21st American Bar Association Reports*. Philadelphia: Dando Printing and Publishing Co., 1898.

Dashiell, J. F. "Experimental Studies of the Influence of Social Situations on the Behavior of Individual Human

Adults," *A Handbook of Social Psychology,* ed. C. Murchison. Worcester, Mass.: Clark University Press, 1935.

Deutsch, M. "Task Structure and Group Process," *American Psychologist,* 6 (1951), 324.

Devlin, Sir Patrick. *Trial by Jury.* Hamlyn Lectures, 8th series. London: Stevens & Sons Ltd., 1956.

Edelstein, David N. "A Kind Word for the Civil Jury," 17 *NACCA Law Journal* 302 (May, 1956).

Festinger, Leon, Stanley Schacter and Kurt Back. *Social Pressures in Informal Groups.* New York: Harper & Brothers, 1950.

Forsyth, William. *History of Trial by Jury,* New Ed. (Morgan). New York: James Cockcroft & Co., 1875.

Grace, H. A. "Effects of Different Degrees of Knowledge About an Audience on the Content of Communication," *Journal of Social Psychology,* 34 (1951), 111.

Gurnee, H. "A Comparison of Collective and Individual Judgments of Fact," *Journal of Experimental Psychology,* 21 (1937), 106.

Holbrook, James G. "Role of Juries in Judicial Administration," *A Survey of Metropolitan Trial Courts—Los Angeles Area.* Los Angeles: Parker & Sons, Inc., 1956.

Holdsworth, Sir William. *A History of English Law,* Vol. I, 7th Ed., rev. ed., Goodhart and Hanbury. London: Methuen & Co., Ltd., 1956.

Jenness, A. "The Role of Discussion in Changing Opinion Regarding A Matter of Fact," *Journal of Abnormal & Social Psychology,* 27 (1932), 279.

Kalven, Jr., Harry. "Report on the Jury Project," *Conference on Aims and Methods of Legal Research,* ed. A. F. Conard. Ann Arbor: The University of Michigan Law School, 1955.

Kelley, H. H. and John W. Thibaut. "Experimental Studies of Group Problem Solving and Process," *Handbook of*

Social Psychology, ed. G. Lindzey. Cambridge, Mass.: Addison-Wesley Publishing Co., Inc., 1954.
Martin, W. S. "The Role of a Jury in a Civil Case," *Jury Trials*. Special Lectures of the Law Society of Upper Canada. Toronto: Richard De Boos Limited, 1959.
Shartel, Burke. "Our Legal System and How It Operates," *Michigan Legal Studies*. Ann Arbor: The University of Michigan Law School, 1951.
Shaw, M. E. "A Comparison of Individuals and Small Groups in the Rational Solution of Complex Problems," *American Journal of Psychology*, 44 (1932), 491.
Sherif, Muzafer. *A Study of Some Social Factors in Perception*. New York: Archives of Psychology (No. 187) (Columbia University), 1935.
Sunderland, Edson R. "Trial by Jury," 11 *University of Cincinnati Law Review* 120 (1937).
———. "Verdicts, General and Special," 29 *Yale Law Journal* 253 (Jan., 1920).
Taylor, D. and W. Faust. "20 Questions—Efficiency in Problem Solving as a Function of Size of Group," *Journal of Experimental Psychology*, 44 (1952), 360.
Thorndike, R. L. "The Effect of Discussion upon the Correctness of Group Decisions, When the Factor of Majority Influence Is Allowed For," *Journal of Social Psychology*, 9 (1938), 343.
Timmons, W. M. "Decisions and Attitudes as Outcomes of the Discussion of a Social Problem," *Contributions to Education*, No. 777. New York: Columbia University Bureau of Publications, 1939.
Tocqueville, de, Alexis. *Democracy in America*, Vol. I, 2nd Ed. Trans. Henry Reeve; ed. Francis Bowen. Cambridge, Mass.: Sever and Francis, 1863.
"Use of Majority Verdicts in the United States," 33 *Journal of the American Judicature Society* 111 (Dec., 1949).
Vanderbilt, Arthur T. *Judges and Jurors: Their Functions,*

Qualifications and Selection. Boston: Boston University Press, 1956.

Watson, G. B. "Do Groups Think More Efficiently Than Individuals?" *Journal of Abnormal & Social Psychology,* 23 (1928), 328.

Zeisel, Hans, Harry Kalven, Jr., and Bernard Buchholz. *Delay in the Court.* Boston: Little, Brown & Company, 1959.